A Passion for Angling

A Passion for Angling

Chris Yates • Bob James • Hugh Miles

Illustrations by Rodger McPhail

Published jointly by
MERLIN UNWIN BOOKS / BBC BOOKS

This book is published to accompany the television series entitled *A Passion for Angling* which was first broadcast in autumn 1993.

Published jointly by
BBC Books,
a division of BBC Enterprises Ltd,
Woodlands,
80 Wood Lane,
London W12 OTT
and
Merlin Unwin Books,
21 Corve Street,
Ludlow,
Shropshire SY8 1DA.

First published in 1993.

ISBN 0 563 36741 5

Illustrations by Rodger McPhail, and Clare Hatcher *(half-title page)*
Photographs by Bob James, Chris Yates and Hugh Miles
Typeset and edited by Merlin Unwin Books
Set in Caslon
Jacket printed by Lawrence Allen Limited, Weston-super-Mare
Printed and bound in Great Britain by Butler & Tanner Limited
Frome, Somerset

CONTENTS

A PASSION FOR ANGLING
by Chris Yates

The Authors

CHRIS YATES, the principal author of this book, has written extensively in the angling press and is the author of *Casting at the Sun* (Pelham, 1986), *The Deepening Pool* (Unwin Hyman, 1990), and *The Secret Carp* (Merlin Unwin Books, 1992). He is the holder of the record for Britain's largest stillwater fish: a monstrous 51½lb mirror carp which he caught in 1980 from Redmire Pool. For 25 years he was a professional  freelance photograper, twice winning Music Week awards for producing the 'best classical record cover of the year'. Now, he devotes all his time to writing and broadcasting. He has made many radio broadcasts, including one for Radio 4 in which he described his favourite carp lake. Fishing has always been a compulsion for him. He lives, with his wife Clare and four children, in a Wiltshire village, close to his favourite river, the Avon.

BOB JAMES is well-known to anglers as a regular contributor to *Improve Your Coarse Fishing*, *Angler's Mail* and *Coarse Fishing*. He is an experienced lecturer, in the past at the London School of Economics, the NRA and the Institute of Fisheries Management, now, to the many fishing clubs and societies in Britain, France and Belgium. He has been described as 'the best all-round angler in Britain'

with many big-fish catches to his name. He no longer makes his living from vintage cars and playing jazz, but instead writes about fishing and is developing considerable skills as a photographer. In fact, many of the photos appearing in this book are his. He lives in a small Wiltshire village with his wife Jan, his back door conveniently overlooking the Avon.

HUGH MILES is a professional film-maker and has been responsible for many award-winning films including *Flight of the Condor* and *The Great Wood of Caledon*. His *Kingdom of the Ice Bear* won an EMMY in America and was the subject of a bestselling book (BBC Books, 1985), as well as being nominated for six British Academy Awards. He has also written *The Track of the Wild Otter* (Elm Tree, 1984) and *The*

Great Wood of Caledon (Colin Baxter, 1991). He is a five-times winner of awards for photography and production at the International Wildlife Film and Television Festival, Wildscreen. As he describes in the opening section of this book, he has nurtured the idea of making a film about angling since 1968, and now at last his dream has come to fruition in *A Passion for Angling*. He lives in Dorset with his wife Sue and children Katie and Peter.

Our Special Thanks

There are some unknown diseases that should carry a government health warning and this book is about one of them. It tells the story of how the germ of an idea that infected us three passionate anglers grew to become an obsession from which we suffered for more than four years.

Contracting the disease was simple. All we had to do was decide to make a short fishing film together. But once afflicted with the creative urge, the only cure seemed to be to make a series of six one-hour films - which is not short at all!

As a result of this painful and expensive remedy, none of us will be quite the same again, but as we attempt to convalesce on the riverbank, we can reflect on the kindness that so many people have shown us during the time when our affliction was most acute.

The book and films recount a series of fishing stories and those closest to the events will probably remember that some of them are even true! They are true because Bob and Chris' skill, patience and dedication enabled them to catch many wonderful fish, though this was not always our priority when we went out filming. How and what we decided to present on angling was very much a distillation of our combined ideas but if we did have separate roles, they might be described as the three Ps - Hugh provided the pence, Bob the places and Chris the poetry. The distinctions were, of course, very blurred, for we all drank the wine!

In presenting angling through the seasons, we tried to present the most idyllic watery landscapes and due to the alarming current tendency of so many fishing clubs to 'tidy up' the countryside, these lovely unspoilt fisheries tend to survive only on private estates. The fact that we were allowed to film on these estates was a privilege we shall never forget, and it is through the generosity of so many landowners that we are able to share our experiences with others. They, of course, wish to preserve their privacy, so we are unable to name them here. But they know of our gratitude in being allowed to share the beauty of the landscapes they work so hard to preserve.

Many others have contributed to our enjoyment, not least the many riverkeepers and gillies who provided us with so much guidance, entertaining company and cups of tea. Of these, Mike Trowbridge has been a constant source of encouragement while also so busy doing much to aid the recovery of fish stocks on the famous Hampshire Avon.

Many tackle companies provided us with superb gear to aid our fish-catching and if one is to be singled out, it would be Peter Drennan, for he has been supportive of our efforts in both word and deed. Incurable romantic Chris refused to use new-fangled gear such as carbon fibre rods of course, but he also refused to return the beautiful prototype split-cane rod that Edward Barder had designed for him, delaying the launch of Edward's rod-building enterprise until filming of that episode was complete.

Apart from tackle from the likes of Drennan, Shimano, Barder and Swallow, we have also received much moral support from the angling press and we do appreciate the privileged role we find ourselves in by being able to present 'our version' of angling on BBC2. We also appreciate the responsibility, and we hope we haven't let any of our fishing friends down.

In putting book and films together we have been lucky to be surrounded by a wonderful team. There are film editors Jill Garrett, Ron Martin, Dave Dickie and Mark Fletcher; then Tom Poore, Julie Mitchell and Graham Wild's constant support. Richard Margoschis and John Kirby have provided much evocative sound and this has been enhanced by Jennie Muskett's beautiful music which Trevor Barber blended together with great skill and patience. Finally, Bernard Cribbins has been a delight to work with. Hardly 'work' really, as he too shares our passion for angling.

So too our long-suffering publisher Merlin, who had the unenviable task of welding thoughts, images and words into something we hope our kind helpers will be pleased to receive as a gift. And there are many to whom we need to say thank you.

Lighting the Fire

An Introduction by Hugh Miles

ABOVE: *A rudd displays its spectacular red and silver livery*

LEFT: *Getting an angle on the story: Hugh in the Redmire punt*

*T*he monastic grounds were encircled by high walls, the gates locked; a prison for an adventurous boy. But such barriers were of little consequence to a child bent on escape and the dormitory was still dark as he stuffed pillows and clothes into his bed to simulate a sleeping presence. The only way out was through a small sidegate beyond the headmaster's lawned garden so, despite the risk of leaving wheel tracks in the dew, he pushed his tackle-laden bike to freedom.

Summer dawns in the Fens were not to be missed when a pre-baited swim bubbled with bream and tench. But all too abruptly on those magical mornings, when the old cane rod creaked with fighting fish, the process of escape had to be reversed before a snooping prefect discovered the subterfuge.

An hour later, this same fair-haired boy with pure voice and angelic features was dressed in the white robes of a cathedral chorister, singing to an admiring congregation. Little did they know that he was not smiling for the joys of God or Monteverdi, but for the inspiration of the capture of his first big roach. It was these escapades into the wild Fens that changed a normal boy with a future career in music to one with an undying passion for fishing and natural history and a determination to be a wildlife film-maker.

Well, I did become that wildlife film-maker, but I still remember vividly those childhood adventures around Ely Cathedral. And that passion for angling still burns brighter than ever.

A three-year course followed school, and my first film was naturally about fishing: a story of the legendary Dennis Pye catching a 26lb pike from the Norfolk Broads.

Within a year, my first freelance assignment was a film called *Tackle and Tactics*. It involved Dennis Pye again and, among other well-known anglers of the day, Peter Stone. Thus encouraged, I hatched plans to make a fishing series with Richard Walker. We even met to discuss how to proceed but, with unfortunate timing, I got a job in the BBC Film Unit and instead of filming fishing, I found myself shooting *Z Cars*, *Dr Who*, *Morecambe and Wise*, *The Two Ronnies*, and going on expeditions with David Attenborough.

Despite the many attractions of 'life with the stars', that unmade fishing series still beckoned. Since then, various attempts have been made to capture angling on television: they've ranged from the disappointing to the downright awful. Television so often fails to convey those elusive ingredients that give angling its captivating magic. But I remained convinced of angling's potential appeal to a wide audience and the admirable John Wilson series, *Go Fishing*, has recently proved that such an audience exists.

So, for 25 years, I have harboured this burning ambition to make another fishing film, and it was through some unlikely twists of fate (that seem so necessary when creating that mysterious alchemy that makes rewarding friendships) that I found myself sharing a pot of tea with Chris Yates and Bob James. It was soon obvious that there was remarkable harmony in our whole approach to the sport.

Firstly, we agreed that a fishing film *must* appeal to the 'hardcore' anglers - obvious you'd think, but this is seldom achieved. Secondly, it must show that there is more to angling than catching fish, so the beauty of the waterside and wildlife must be included.

Thirdly, it should not stress 'how to catch' but rather 'how to enjoy'. This combination of elements would, we felt sure, appeal to a wide audience. And as a bonus, we had Bob and Chris' terrific sense of humour. We hoped it would survive the test of having to catch fish for the camera.

Past experience making wildlife films convinced me that the best way to capture all these elements, *and* the fish, was to be a film crew of one. So we decided that just the three of us would try to make a half-hour film on carp fishing, with famous Redmire Pool as the first location. We wanted to start filming just before the opening of the fishing season, so that we could observe the fish and wildlife undisturbed. However, the first week at Redmire is much sought-after and it was to be auctioned at the Carp Society's AGM. I was away filming wildlife in Africa, so we agreed that Bob and Chris were to bid up to £1,000, which we felt would be more than adequate.

When they broke the news they'd got the week's fishing, I was delighted. Less so when they told me they had to bid £2,000! They hardly dared tell me that the previous two opening weeks of the season had produced a total catch of nil, but in Bob and Chris we had the necessary talent to fulfil our objectives. Bob had an enviable record of specimen fish to his name, including many big carp - and, to enliven proceedings, a ready wit. Chris knew Redmire well, having caught Britain's record carp of $51\frac{1}{2}$lbs there in 1980. He also had an eloquent tongue and if Bob could get a word in edgeways, their combined banter would surely be entertaining.

So, we were on the verge of trying to capture not just a fish, but that essential magic that had fired our imagination as children. My own beginnings were inauspicious: a small drain that flowed from a pipe into the Great Ouse at Ely. The wall on which I sat was smoothed by the trousers of many small boys who sat, with bamboo rods and small worms, to catch gudgeon or, if we were very lucky, small perch. Then one day, one of the children caught a large roach - well, over half a pound anyway - and that small boy has been literally hooked on the pursuit of big roach ever since. I do still have a soft spot for gudgeon and perch, but hunting big roach has become an obsession.

My own passion for angling was fired by something as simple as a single fish, but what was it that caused Bob and Chris to be equally afflicted? Chris takes up the story...

1

First Casts

by Chris Yates

ABOVE: *Chris and Bob with their childhood hero, Bernard Venables, alias 'Mr Crabtree'*

LEFT: *Sunset on the Avon, the taking time for barbel, as Chris and Peter prepare for their first fish*

I vividly recall my first sight of a big fish - a carp - in my village pond. In all the years I'd known the place, I'd never seen anything bigger than a stickleback but then, one morning, this great golden creature leapt out of the water like a dragon rising out of myth. Not only did it transform the world as I knew it, making the entire landscape suddenly more dramatic and mysterious, it also gave meaning to the local fishermen. I had often watched those strange, silent characters sitting somewhat moodily round the banks and now I finally understood why they always looked so patient and yet seemed to sustain a quiet, contained excitement. After all, it was obviously a grave and serious matter to challenge such a creature as the one I'd seen.

I didn't catch anything when I first cast a line, but it was a day full of colour and tense anticipation. Only when my patience was about to give out - after almost a week without a bite - did I begin to get desperate. Then, acting on a bit of invaluable advice, I eventually caught my very first fish - a glorious gudgeon at least four inches long. It was a wonderful moment and also a fateful one: suddenly, I was a real angler.

Though he grew up in London, this apparent disadvantage didn't stop Bob also becoming an incurable angler from an early age. Many urban environments are nothing but great suffocaters of all but the most organised outdoor pursuits. London, however, with the Thames and all the lakes and ponds in the royal parks and on the commons, has great potential for the angler - as Bob soon discovered.

Later on we take this young minnow-catcher, Peter, fishing for barbel. His enthusiasm echoed our own boyhood dreams

He drew his earliest inspiration from watching the fishermen at Wimbledon Park lake, when he was only two. Later on, he realised he could fish the Thames at Putney or Richmond after school and catch a netful of dace. He could cycle to Hyde Park and catch perch in the Serpentine. He could take a train to Kingston and fish for tench in the Longwater of Hampton Court Park.

In fact it was surprising that he and I didn't meet up sooner, for in our early days - during the late 50s - we must sometimes have been fishing at the same place. Bob lived in south-west London and my village, Burgh Heath, was on the south-west edge of the London suburbs. I would often travel by bus to Surbiton and then take the ferry across the Thames so that I could fish the river from the towpath. This was also one of Bob's favourite casting places. I would also occasionally go through the gate by the ferry landing stage and walk across the park to the Longwater.

In fact the more I think about it the more I'm convinced that the young angler I spoke to 30 years ago, as he played in a wonderful Thames roach, was definitely Bob. He was using a certain rod and reel, fishing in the same style, using the same method, and casting from precisely the same point that Bob has since confirmed were all part of his standard practice at that place. Our paths may have crossed, but they parted again and it wasn't till I moved to my present cottage in 1986, that I met Bob properly.

Through all that time it was our childhood inspirations that encouraged us to keep casting, especially during those rather too regular periods when nothing much was caught. And when we couldn't fish at all, because of school or, later, because we were distracted by a different kind of romance, we'd always be able to fall back on our fishing books. Authors like Bernard Venables, Richard Walker, and 'BB' provided a wonderful instant escape from everyday life. They also encouraged us to believe that we were not completely insane, for these writers too had suffered the same hopes, joys and disappointments as us.

In fact the more I read the more I suspected that all fanatical, dyed-in-the-wool anglers had once dreamed the same improbable boyhood dreams that I had. The only difference was that while I had fantasised about monster carp, others had dreamed of pike or salmon or tench, trout, roach, barbel, or rudd. And, of course,

The moment of truth - a barbel breaks the surface on the Hampshire Avon. Chris and his gillie emerge from cover having ambushed a splendid specimen

many anglers have no special favourite, but regard all species as equally desirable.

When I finally met Bob, it was interesting to discover how similar our particular childhood dreams had been and how faithful we'd been to them through - how long has it been now? Good Grief! Forty years!

I moved home, as Bob had done for the same reason, so that I could live nearer to my favourite river, the Hampshire Avon. We met each other on the banks a few times and then had a day's fishing together, at a famous barbel swim near Fordingbridge. The occasion was memorable not because of the fish (which were behaving churlishly), but because of the talk and the weather. No sooner had we begun casting than the rain began to fall. It came down in torrents for hours and hours - but the talk went on for longer. Furthermore, the talk continued long after we eventually dived for shelter at a local pub, and it burbled on beyond closing time until the landlord finally reminded us of the purpose of his door.

What had given our conversation its relentless vitality was not simply the fact that we were both anglers who liked fishing the same river, but also because it turned out that we'd been fishing in the same sort of way, for the same kinds of fish at the same places - since childhood. We had both spent too much of our lives chasing carp, chub, tench, and now barbel. Moreover, we had both cultivated the same kind of idealised image of the perfect location for each particular species, these images coloured by nostalgic memories or evocative descriptions from our favourite books (passages often remembered by heart).

Of course there were differences too and these became more apparent later on, when we began exploring more of the Avon. In his fishing, Bob is more determined than me, while I am more lackadaisical: we are both instinctive, but he is meticulous and methodical while I am careless and wayward. Bob likes to fish to a game plan while I usually fish on a whim. Also, he still listens to the Beach Boys.

During that first season we fished our way right down the Avon, from Downton to Christchurch, and though there were a few blank days, these were uncommon. It was much more likely that we'd catch not only the fish we were after (usually barbel) but also enjoy an equal amount of success. In fact the synchronisation of our catches began to get rather weird - we would invariably catch the same number of fish and they would often be exactly the same respective weights. However, if we went out after roach or grayling, trout or dace, Bob would completely outfish me.

Though I was obviously aware of his wonderful wildlife films, I didn't realise, before I met him, that Hugh was also as fanatical an angler as we were and had experienced the same kinds of boyhood adventures. I certainly didn't realise that Hugh had nursed a lifelong ambition to make a film inspired by those kinds of adventures - a film imbued with the same sort of spirit as one of our favourite books, *Mr Crabtree Goes Fishing* by Bernard Venables.

Back in his college days, Hugh had actually made a wonderfully atmospheric film about pike with the famous angler Dennis Pye, and later one of his first commissions was to produce a film for the tackle trade with the specimen hunter Peter Stone, and again Dennis Pye. In fact, in his early film-making days, Hugh was on familiar terms with many of the prime movers of the angling world and he even encouraged the late Dick Walker to consider seriously his idea of a fishing epic. If it hadn't been for Dick's untimely death and the fact that Hugh's wildlife projects were orbiting him round the world even more regularly than now, they would definitely have collaborated.

'A glorious gudgeon at least four inches long'

RIGHT: *We didn't realise that Hugh was as fanatical an angler as we were. Even though he is a died-in-the-wool roach angler, Hugh will never forget his magnificent brace of 3lb perch*

Then, years later, during one of his less hectic moments, Hugh had time to read my book *Casting at the Sun*, which helped to rekindle the old dream. I hasten to add that I am not and never shall be in the same mould of fish catching excellence as the Pyes and Stones and Walkers of this world, but still, Hugh saw in the book the same convergence of enthusiasms that were in these people, that were also in Mr Crabtree and were also in him.

In the summer of 1987, Graham Pepler, the owner of Davis Tackle on the Royalty fishery, phoned to invite me to his 40th birthday party, '... and there's a man coming,' said Graham, 'a friend of mine, Hugh Miles, whom I think you should meet. He'd like to discuss a little project he's got in mind.'

This was the first I'd heard of Hugh's idea for a fishing film, but, unfortunately, I couldn't make the party and shortly afterwards Hugh disappeared to Africa to start tracking and filming wild dogs. It wasn't until a year later that we finally met up. Bob, who had often seen Hugh roach fishing on the Avon in winter, managed to arrange a rendezvous at his house and we three had another one of those evenings when the talk was like a river in spate. After the briefest of introductions, we got straight down to 'business'.

We talked about those things that made fishing seem such a necessary pursuit, those fundamentals that we had all known since boyhood and which gave angling its special magic: the mysterious quality of deep water; the expectant look of a painted quill, poised on the surface; the tremor of excitement as a shadow glides through the depths; the beauty of a summer dawn by a still lake; the drama of a river in a winter flood; the widening circle of ripple after a fish has leapt. These were images which would always endure and which never failed to stir our imaginations.

They, and a score of similar glories, were what Hugh hoped to capture on film.

If an angling film could convey the excitement, beauty and mystery of fishing as well as revealing some of its absurdities and eccentricities then it could be hugely entertaining, appealing to an audience of both fishers and non-fishers. But was this possible? And was it worth it?

Being a brilliant cameraman, who had filmed everything from a man falling off a roof (for *Z-Cars* during his days as a BBC cameraman) to a polar bear emerging from a snow hole (for his own

Kingdom of the Ice Bear), Hugh was obviously the best person to attempt such a project, but what about the performers? Hugh thought Bob and I were perfectly capable of fulfilling the roles of complete if quirky anglers, but I felt this was like choosing Bill and Ben to present *Gardener's World*.

As a superb all-rounder, who is equally at home catching trout on the dry fly as he is barbel on legered luncheon meat, Bob obviously had the potential to produce the prize catches that Hugh felt were necessary to reveal the true splendour of the individual species. But over the years, Bob's fishing had become less intense and more enjoyable - less of a challenge and more of a lark: would his angling suffer under the pressure of a film camera?

As I said earlier, because Hugh had read my book, he knew I regarded the watery world in the same slightly golden light as he did and it was this rather than my inconsistent ability to catch big carp that made him believe I was the other man for the job. But would his faith in me survive my multiple casts into overhead branches?

'What you really need, Hugh,' said someone, when we first discussed the film with a wider group of anglers, 'are a couple of real experts.' I thought about this for a while. If you're making a conventional gardening programme then obviously you'll require an expert gardener to present it. But it might be more entertaining if your presenters *were* Bill and Ben.

2

Redmire Legends

*F*our days before the new season began, Bob pulled up next to my cottage, his estate car piled beyond its roof with tackle, bait, provisions, a boat and a bicycle, everything, in fact, except his wife Jan and his dogs. The dogs would have loved to come, but Jan was happy to be left to her gardening.

By the time we'd loaded up with my own gear (and my own bike) the poor car was almost scraping the ground. Three merry people - my wife Clare, daughter Camilla and son Alexander - waved farewell from over the garden hedge as we set off on our first attempt to catch a fish for a film camera.

After numerous discussions with Hugh through the winter and spring of '89 we foolishly agreed that, because so many ideas were developing and getting out of hand, we should attempt a whole series of fishing programmes rather than just a single one, as Hugh had originally envisaged. Each episode would, it was hoped, go to the heart of a particular type of fishing, conveying the essence of, say, a classic tench morning, revealing the characteristics of the waterside and the beauties of the fish as well as the emotional responses of the angler - the excitements, joys and occasional moments of dark despair. And we would show contrasting styles, with Bob epitomising the stylish, well-equipped, modern approach, while I would remain as I am - a simple, incurable traditionalist. But we also agreed, even more foolishly, that we would not go gently into the project, sensibly testing the water and spending a few days with Hugh's camera, fishing at some easy little stream. We would, instead, jump in at the deep end and see if the luck of Isaak Walton came with us: we would try and catch a big carp from Redmire Pool.

What is so deep-ended about that, you might ask, especially if you recall that Redmire is an attractive pool, full of large carp? Surely an experienced film-maker couldn't fail to capture some memorable images, just as two experienced anglers couldn't fail to capture a decent fish? Firstly, no-one could guarantee good weather and as we had only one week's fishing with no possibility of a return visit that season, Hugh was going to find it problematic if the conditions went against us. Secondly, Redmire is a mysterious place.

It may be only three acres, it may have produced the last three record carp as well as scores of twenty and thirty pounders, but there are times when you can walk round its banks and not see a sign of a fish. They have a talent for sudden and complete dematerialisation and whole weeks can pass when an angler's line never even twitches. It was, of course, an advantage having the privilege of first cast of the season, but even that was no guarantee of success. On the opening of the previous two seasons, no-one had a bite.

Whatever the risks, however, we all felt that Redmire was a great choice of venue. If we wanted to capture the essence of real carp angling, with all its potential for high drama, its unique mix of intensity and tranquillity, where better than at carp fishing's most historic, most famous water?

If we succeeded, if Hugh got enough material to create a half hour programme equal to his normal extremely high standards, then perhaps we might go on to other waters and other fishes.

OVERLEAF: *Midsummer sunrise at Redmire. 'As the sun rose, turning the mist golden, Hugh, Bob and I drank tea under the oaks'*

BELOW: *'He had that alert look about him and I guessed he was interested in breakfast'*

And if we failed; if we didn't catch anything and it rained every day; if we ended up getting on each other's nerves and finally pushed each other in; then we could simply forget the whole crazy idea and go back to whatever we'd been doing before.

It certainly wasn't raining when Bob and I arrived at Redmire that first morning. The sky was blue, the sun bright and the air had that reassuring stillness and density that promised settled weather. The pool looked exquisite with its beautifully over-grown banks starred with dog rose, and elder blossom. It smelt sweeter than a tropical greenhouse. It must have been midday when we arrived, but Hugh had been there since early morning spending the intervening hours creeping quietly about, watching and familiarising himself with Redmire's special character.

When we met on the banks he had the appearance of some-one who had just stumbled on paradise. 'It's all looking splendid!'

he said. And even I, who had first seen Redmire twenty years previously and who knew her in all kinds of weather, seasons and moods, had to admit that I had never seen her looking so lovely.

Hugh and Bob had visited Redmire just once before, on our reconnaissance trip six weeks earlier, when only the willows were in leaf and only the dandelions in flower. It looked pretty enough then, but that was just a watercolour sketch compared to this radiant midsummer masterpiece.

'Have you seen any carp?', asked Bob.

'Seen any carp!' said Hugh. 'You couldn't miss them even if you tried. They're spawning!'

He led us along the bank, away from the deeps up to the shallows where the fish were charging and cavorting madly about, completely oblivious to the rest of the world. They churned up great fountains of spray and sent huge ripples wheeling across the pool as the packs of males pursued the much larger females. Many of the carp were over 20lbs and, though we didn't see anything extravagantly huge, it was a dramatic and unique enough spectacle to switch Hugh instantly into filming mode. He went and fetched his camera and tripod and must have shot two reels by tea-time.

It was obviously a good idea to have a few days to prepare ourselves before the actual fishing began. We spent a lot of time drinking tea or wine, sitting on the banks and discussing worst case and best case scenarios. The former usually centred round the quite likely prospect of having just one chance between us in the entire week. This chance, it's true, led to the hooking of a monster carp, but the fish was ultimately lost when the angler was struck by lightning. The best case scenario entailed 20-pounders each for Bob and me and then a new record fish for Hugh while he was taking a break from filming.

As well as dreaming, we naturally planned the logistics of our venture. Bob and I helped Hugh build a scaffold tower next to the shallows, giving his camera a heron's eye view of the carp below, cruising, basking or feeding in crystal clear water. Hugh also set up camouflaged hides so that he could film Redmire's other wildlife, the coots, moorhens, ducks and grebes. We watched the behaviour of the fish and tried to surmise where our best chances lay, and of course we offered them all kinds of tasty sweetmeats and watched their reactions.

Though I hadn't fished Redmire for eight years, it didn't appear - once the carp had finished spawning - that their habits had changed much. They still came up to the shallows to feed in the evenings, making enormous rose-shaped clouds of mud as they truffled for larvae. And they continued to bask in the midday sun at their favourite place, in the weedbeds off the islands. At dawn they would usually feed in margins along the west bank, just as they had always done - as long as they didn't suspect an angler's presence.

Knowing the pool intimately for so many years, I had an obvious advantage over Bob who, as I said, had only seen the place once before. However, Bob had great faith in his methods and baits and after a couple of days, we knew this location wasn't going to be a problem. Also, as I had carp fished with him for years, I knew Bob would bend a rod eventually, whatever happened.

Our confidence began to grow even more when we realised how enthusiastically the carp were approaching our groundbait.

A Redmire serpent. The old English name for a grass snake was the water snake

Furthermore, they were taking food from the surface which was something of a novelty among such confirmed bottom feeders. Redmire carp have always been famous for their refusal to look up when they are hungry.

The conditions remained perfect, with radiant sunrises, glorious blue skies, gentle breezes (just enough to stir the very tops of the trees) flamboyant sunsets and soft, still, luminous nights.

On the evening of 15 June, Hugh, Bob and I were sitting on the dam ready to mark the opening of the new season. At the stroke of midnight a champagne cork and a signal rocket rose simultaneously into the starry sky. We toasted the good name of Isaak Walton and asked that he should bring us luck. And naturally we raised a glass to Redmire and hoped she was feeling generous. Then we cast our lines into the dark water, all three of us, and fished for just an hour, though it was purely a symbolic act and we didn't honestly expect any instant response. At one o'clock Hugh retired to his tent under the oaks for a short sleep while Bob and I crept off along the banks settling quietly down in the pitches we'd prepared earlier, praying that the carp were still as eager for our baits as they'd been before.

Bob had set up stall halfway along the east bank, near two towering balsam poplars. He had baited an area along the edge of a weedbed, 30 yards away. The water was deep immediately in front of him, but it became gradually shallower where the weedbed began and the fish had been constantly patrolling in that area. So it was there that he cast two identical sets of tackle and then sat back to await the dawn. I tiptoed up to the shallows and listened to the silence, hoping to hear it either gently or abruptly broken by the swirl or leap of a big carp. On really quiet nights it is actually possible to hear the 'fizz' of bubbles when a fish is delving for blood-worms, but they have to be reasonably close, within 20 or 30 feet.

But, on that night, there was no evidence of carp at all, just the usual nocturnal stirrings of voles and mice, the faint call of an owl, the thin squeaking of young moorhens. Overhead, the stars glimmered brightly, but their reflections became lost in the gradually thickening mist.

I made a speculative cast from beneath the spreading branches of an old ash tree and the bait hadn't been in place for

more than an hour when the new day began. The stars faded overhead and the trees along the eastern skyline seemed more densely black against the growing light. Still no movement of carp - they had obviously been studying their calendars and we probably wouldn't see them again for the rest of the week.

As the sun rose, turning the mist golden, Hugh, Bob and I drank tea under the oaks. It was going to be another lovely day, a day of sultry heat, blue skies, bird song, tranquillity - but not complete tranquillity because, at around one o'clock, there was going to be an almighty splash and a great carp (that hadn't been watching the calendar) would come rolling over the net. It happened thus:

A group of fish came up from deep water to feed in the weedy area of shallows at the south-west corner of the dam. I watched them as they sent up great pinkish clouds of disturbed mud and such was their enthusiasm for lunch they didn't notice me at all as I carefully waded into the margins and cast across to them, dropping the bait just under the dam wall. They didn't notice Hugh either, as he crept into position on the dam itself, half hidden by hazel bushes and zoomed in on a patch of bubbles. We had a little while to wait, but it seemed certain that something would happen and, eventually, my line trembled and drew taut and, with a flick of the wrist, I'd hooked the first Redmire carp of the season.

It burst out of the corner and went deep and far towards the centre of the pool. I waded out from beneath the overhanging trees so that I could get a better angle of pull and tried to steer it round towards me, the old cane rod making a glorious curve. (I must mention here that the rod really was quite ancient: it also happened to be the most famous carp rod in history. It was designed and made in 1951 by Richard Walker, who used it to catch his celebrated 44-pounder in September 1952. After that it was auctioned to raise money for the Angler's Cooperative Association and had been in a glass case for 30 years before being offered, via C. Derbyshire Ball, to the Golden Scale Club. Therefore, this was its first visit to Redmire since it subdued the 'forty-four'.)

Bob had just moved pitch further up the pool, but he heard my shout and came suddenly onto the scene to act as gillie. For a while the carp cocooned itself in a deep weed bed, but I eased it

OVERLEAF: *Our Trojan horse. Kevin, the scarecrow, lulling the Redmire carp into a false sense of security*

free and it came grudgingly towards us, finally rolling on the surface just a yard beyond Bob's reach. We did no more than just wait, unmoving, both leaning forward a little, as the fish wallowed nearer, nearer - then, with a last lunge, a final swirl and an ounce of extra pressure, it came over the mesh. Bob lifted, there was a violent splash and we had what the producer had asked for: a 20lb common carp.

Hugh was delighted. He'd got the entire sequence on film and concluded it with some glowing close-ups of the fish, a beautiful specimen of exactly 24lbs.

'Cue bottle of celebration claret,' he said after it had swum out of camera-range and disappeared back into the depths.

Bob was becoming mildly perplexed. The carp had seemed

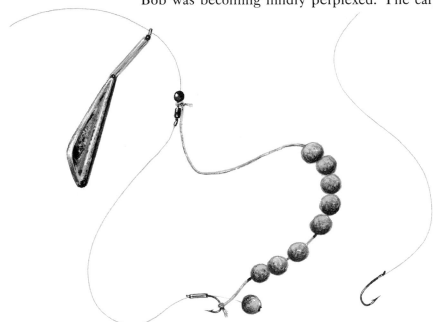

OF BOILIES AND WATER-SOLUBLE STRINGS

There is a trend nowadays to view carp fishing as a kind of science. Anglers spend days perfecting mind-boggling flavour additives to mix with their baits, or developing increasingly complex and confusing hook rigs - some of them, in our view, distinctly unethical, although Bob points out that they are no more devious than a barb on a hook. The carp themselves are regarded as almost mechanical objects who respond predictably to given circumstances; their mystery and beauty eclipsed by these outlandish theories and ever more efficient and sophisticated techniques.

The weird tackle arrangement illustrated here, with its swivels, rubber tubing, unbaited hook and free offerings secured by water-soluble string, is a typical standard rig for modern carp fishing. Traditionalists, like me, take heart from the fact that carp can still be caught by the simplest methods, and the simplest method of all - just the hook and line - caught the biggest carp in Britain, my 51½-pounder from Redmire.

so approachable, so 'easy' and yet, though he knew fish were passing close to his baits, they were politely ignoring them. He was using all the most advanced carp angling techniques and he knew his specially-manufactured baits were of proven quality, but it appeared that the carp had seen his tricks before. 'What's the secret?,' he asked when I came round to his pitch to see how he was faring. 'Luck,' I replied, and though of course this was not strictly true, we had a long discussion on the value of good fortune. Because this began to develop into a friendly, no-holds barred, cudgels and gaffs argument on the difference between Bob's scientific and my non-scientific approach, Hugh asked for a moment's silence while he set up his camera again. Such talk, said Hugh, might make a useful conversational interlude to the filming. But the debate was just starting up again, helped along by a famous quote from H.T. Sheringham ('I take my stand entirely on luck'), when Bob's line began to spill from the reel.

It was another big carp. There was a great swirl and the fish headed along the edge of a weedbed towards an overhanging willow on our right. Bob held it firmly and for a while the fish simply bored and circled on the bottom. But then it made a more powerful lunge for sanctuary and Bob had to give line. There were all kinds of snaking roots and branches under the bank and it seemed likely that the carp was going to do something mischievous.

At the last moment, however, Bob leaned right out, laid the rod over and managed to sidestrain the fish clear. Then it was a long hauling match back towards him. I passed him the net, he wound down and with sighs of relief and cheers all round, brought another sparkling 20lb common safely onto the bank.

Incredibly, this fish was also exactly 24lbs. Moreover, I identified it as being the same fish I had caught almost 20 years earlier when it was, similarly, my own first big Redmire carp. The lack of both pelvic fins made it instantly recognisable. It was wonderful that this near-60-year-old carp was still flourishing. And just now, at the time of writing, I hear that this same specimen has recently been landed again, at a weight of over 26lbs, so it is still growing!

We didn't think we had quite enough wine and champagne and rockets for a proper celebration and so, after releasing the resplendent creature, we went off to spend the evening at the local pub.

One of the problems I used to encounter at Redmire was the irritating habit of junior carp acting as escorts to their lords and masters. Almost every big fish approaching its feeding grounds on the shallows would be accompanied by a group of smaller carp, like remora attached to a shark. The problem, of course, was that any bait cast towards the patriarch would nearly always get snaffled by one of its escorts - fish of between five and ten pounds. The resulting commotions would then cause the monster to disappear from the scene altogether. While it was possible to present a bait directly to a large fish if it came in close enough and to withdraw the bait if a small carp suddenly nosed down for it, the group was usually just too far away for the angler to see exactly what was going on. And so the already small chance of hooking a monster was further diminished.

For years I pondered over this quandary, wondering how I could always guarantee to drop a bait directly on the nose of the largest fish in sight. And then, one day, when I was watching a group of carp basking next to an old half-sunken tree stump, I thought of Kevin the aquatic scarecrow.

It was a simple two-part idea. In Plan A, Kevin would stand for three days in the middle of the shallows, dressed in my coat and hat, holding my rod. On each day I would scatter groundbait all round him and the carp would, after a period of inevitable wariness and suspicion, come to accept him not just as part of their surroundings but as a mysterious provider of food. In Plan B, the biggest carp to approach Kevin would suddenly find itself hooked. Unfortunately, though I fished Redmire regularly from 1972-81, I didn't dream this idea up until my last year and then never had an opportunity to put it into practice. But on my return this time, with the conditions ideal for such an experiment and Hugh keen to break with convention whenever possible, Kevin was finally dressed for the part and Plan A went into operation.

Within two days Hugh was able to film over a dozen carp feeding unconcernedly round the scarecrow. In fact there was even a moment when a large fish sidled right up to it and rubbed its flank on the support pole, making Kevin's hat quiver.

While Plan A was happening at the upper end of the pool, Bob and I were fishing at the other end, sitting on the dam trying to catch gudgeon. Now the gudgeon is a very small and rather daft little creature and it was the perfect anodyne to fish for him

after an intense night's carp angling. With light float tackle and a single maggot on a tiny hook it was possible to catch a fish a cast, but on that particular morning the gudgeon were not feeling generous.

While we were savouring the first pot of tea of the day, Bob caught two and I caught one. During the second pot only one float went under - mine. We finished our tea and Bob said we should reel in before one of us spoilt the fishing by catching more than the other, but just then my float again dipped under and out came my third gudgeon. So I put the kettle on again for another pot and we got stuck into a proper gudgeon match. However, just as Bob's float began to quiver expectantly, I spotted a carp's head slowly rising up in a distant weed bed. It seemed to have taken something from the surface. 'Time's up!' I announced. 'Match over.' 'No it's not,' said Bob. 'We were going to fish through a third pot, remember?' 'We'll just have to cancel the tea,' I said. 'But the match is only suspended,' warned Bob. 'We'll restart tomorrow, at dawn!'

I grabbed my carp rod and scuttled off along the bank towards the place where the carp had risen, near one of Redmire's little islands. After crossing to it over a plank bridge, I scanned the surrounding weed bed with binoculars and there, in a little gap of open water, was the big blueish shape of a 20-pounder. He wasn't simply basking, semi-comatose in the morning sun; he had a quietly alert look about him and I guessed he was still interested in breakfast.

Before casting, I sneaked off and told Hugh about the potential for a bit of drama. We had, of course, agreed that Hugh must be made aware of such a situation before it began to happen. As he was a one man crew - film cameraman and sound recordist - there were always various technical considerations to attend to, prior to the action. But, being a fisherman, Hugh realised the importance of speed and quiet - he knows that great angling opportunities don't present themselves for long, and having spent a lifetime stalking wildlife with a film camera, he knows how to move soundlessly.

Monkey business: it takes a good head for heights to attain this level of carp fishing

Therefore it was only a few moments before everything was ready and I could cast a floating bait - two pre-soaked dog biscuits - just beyond the still-lingering carp. I waited a second, then gently retrieved the bait so that it drifted directly over the fish's head. But instead of coming straight up and taking it, the carp swam leisurely away, moving in a half circle and appearing to sniff its way to the point where the bait had originally landed. If only I'd let it lie! Cursing under my breath, I watched the fish gradually dematerialise beneath the floating weedbeds.

It's always a mistake, though, once a carp has seen your bait, refused it and departed, to simply retrieve and recast elsewhere. Four times out of ten - which in carp fishing terms amounts to predictable behaviour - the fish will return and inspect the bait again. And four times out of a hundred he will then take it, which in carp fishing terms is an overwhelmingly enthusiastic response. Don't forget, also, that I had never taken a big carp from the surface at Redmire, so I was doubly delighted when, after a tense wait in the hot sun, the fish reappeared below the bait and took it decisively. There was a gigantic swirl when I struck and the entire weedbed seemed to spiral down after a vanishing tail. The first powerdive of a big carp never fails to astonish me.

Because of the density of weed, there were no spectacularly long runs or rapid changes of direction, but it was still a terrific tussle, with several explosive eruptions of water and a final moment of crisis when the fish wrapped me round an unyielding clump of weedstems. Trying to stay calm while varying the pressure and direction of pull, I gradually eased the carp out of its sanctuary and within another few seconds it was rolling and plunging into the net.

It was $23\frac{1}{2}$lbs, another fully-scaled fish and undoubtedly one of the most beautiful carp I've ever caught, like moulded gold.

Back at base camp that evening, under the old oaks at the south-east corner of the pool, Hugh served up a delicious supper accompanied by a bottle of fine claret. And as we watched the sunset through our wine glasses we all agreed that Isaak was looking after us rather well. The weather was still blissful, the carp were being unusually co-operative and Hugh had filmed some wonderful sequences. Already he had more material 'in the can' than he'd hoped for and we were only halfway through our stay. 'But you haven't filmed a gudgeon match yet!' said Bob.

LEFT: *The musical trillings of the dabchicks filled the twilight hours at Redmire*

Next morning, at dawn, Bob and I boarded the Redmire punt, and paddled out into the rising mist and continued our gudgeon match - to the death. Well, it felt like death, having rolled out of our sleeping bags so early, with the effects of last night's claret obscuring vision and not even time enough for a restorative cup of tea. The sun was just coming up (at about 5am) and Hugh wanted us silhouetted against it, having decided to add our whimsical sideshow to his film. However, I had my reward in the end, even though Bob beat me by the greatest margin in the history of gudgeon angling. We had a bottle of champagne for the winner and he was generous enough to share it. The toast, naturally, was to Redmire.

For the first and only time during our stay, the sky slowly filled with cloud and the pool temporarily lost its sparkle. But we didn't mind, we'd already done enough filming for one day, the lowering light would encourage the carp to feed even better than before and Hugh was eager to have a proper cast. So far, he'd only managed a few brief angling intervals between film-spools, usually at dawn, when Bob and I were still asleep. He'd had a few chances, though; one when stalking a big fish on the shallows and twice when creeping up on carp in his own 'secret swim' - under a curtain of honeysuckle near Inghams Pitch. Each time, he'd managed to connect with his quarry, but each time the fish had escaped, either breaking the line or slipping the hook. On that cloudy day, though, Hugh had more time to prepare. Finding his secret swim deserted, he crept onto the island and baited the margins with 'magic powder' (some kind of stock salmon feed). Then he flicked out a float-fished worm and within minutes the carp had moved in.

It was a nice coincidence that I sneaked up behind him to see how he was doing at the precise moment that his float slid gracefully away. This time the fish didn't escape and after a close struggle, with Hugh's old MK IV Avon dangerously hooped, I netted his first Redmire carp - a shining, fully-scaled fish, just under 10lbs.

Fishing the shallows, also with a float, Bob hooked a much bigger carp. It raced halfway down the pool, was turned and then, just as it began to come in, rolled off the hook. Also from the shallows, and not far from the scarecrow, I landed a common of just over 10lbs. Then it was time for tea.

Sleeping quarters at Redmire: a lie-in after a hard night's fishing

The next day was an almost eerie catalogue of disasters. Everything went wrong. Before it was light Bob got weeded by a really large fish and went out in the punt to try and net it. He failed. Also he had a rather bad experience with the pool itself: 'I suddenly felt it wanted to murder me!' he said. Then Hugh found a group of carp feeding under the overhanging oak - where we'd never seen a fish before. He was just going to creep up on them when the door of his nearby car slammed mysteriously shut. Exit carp.

Hugh wanted to deliver his film for processing after breakfast, but his car wouldn't start. The battery was flat. That hadn't happened to him before. So Bob got some jump leads, but couldn't find his car keys. And Bob never loses his keys! Eventually Hugh set off for Gloucester and Bob and I decided we'd better only fish for gudgeon. Unfortunately I used Hugh's favourite Hardy roach rod, hooked a carp and broke the tip. (Well, it *was* a carbon rod!) After that we thought we'd better not fish at all and spent the rest of the day hurling a frisbee across the surrounding fields - though not before making a formal apology to Redmire. It seemed we had offended her in some way, perhaps by taking her too much for granted. So we begged forgiveness and left her in peace for a while. (It took more than an apology before Hugh forgave me for breaking his rod! Was it six cases of vintage port or a new crow-quill float? I don't quite recall.)

We agreed, next day, that it was time for Plan B. Hugh went up his scaffold tower with the camera, Bob joined him, sensing the prospect of a good laugh, and, while the carp were off the shallows, Kevin and I swopped places. To anyone, or any fish, who hadn't witnessed the switch, the scene would have remained unchanged: the willow-fringed shallows remained guarded by a scarecrow dressed in an old riding coat, a battered straw hat and holding a split-cane rod. However, the line from the rod had now been baited and it was going to be a simple matter to lower the bunch of maggots in front of the first big carp to come up and see me. And there was a smattering of fresh groundbait round my feet. But would the fish - the best-educated carp in England - be deceived?

After an hour of waiting I had sunk a little deeper into the lake bed and the water was lapping over the top of my waders. The late afternoon sun felt uncomfortably warm and a fly was beginning to annoy me, buzzing continually round my head. But I couldn't move to wave it away because, not far down the pool, I could see a bow wave. Gradually, a big carp materialised out of the surface glare. Soon I could see it in every detail; the fine scaling, like chain mail, the barely moving, wing-like pectorals, the furling, half-erect dorsal. I even saw the twitch of the revolving eye sockets as the fish switched focus from the lake bed to his old friend Kevin. I'm sure he wanted to say hello. It had worked! The carp was completely fooled. It appeared he had no suspicions at all, and yet, had I been standing bolt upright like that on the bank, rod in hand, he would have fled as soon as he saw me.

At least a dozen smaller carp were slowly following in his wake and within a few minutes I could count 18 fish casually browsing on the groundbait under my nose. I hardly dared breathe, but I couldn't help smiling.

Out of the corner of my eye I noticed a different kind of movement and, keeping my position fixed, looked up to see Bob and Hugh making impatient casting motions from the top of the tower. Idiot! I'd become so immersed in the grand deception that I'd forgotten I was meant to be fishing. As I was wearing my radio mike I was also meant to be delivering a whispered commentary. So, only fractionally moving the rod tip, I waited for the right moment and then lowered the bait under the big carp's nose.

Everything had worked so well up to that moment that I was almost shocked when the fish refused the offer. He drifted away with such a disdainful expression that I thought he must have twigged me. Another carp - a fish of about 15lbs - nosed down for the bait and I decided, just for the film's sake, to let him take it. I was so blasé and over-confident that I completely missed on the strike. Yet surprisingly, despite my sudden movement, I still didn't arouse any suspicions in the other carp. One or two flinched and turned, but they were soon feeding on my groundbait again.

Then the big one - a fish in the high twenties - returned and

OPPOSITE: *The Redmire
punt is moored in
readiness for the historic
gudgeon match*

this time he took the bait confidently and the strike was successful. Bow waves went out in every direction as the fish scattered.
The biggest wave of all headed directly towards a weedbed and I
couldn't slow it down. There was a volcanic splash and then a
sickening jolt as the line went slack. The hook had slipped and I
was left standing rather droopily in the shallows, muttering
pathetically.

After such a Trojan betrayal every carp disappeared into the
depths and we didn't see scale nor fin of them for the rest of the
day.

Despite the loss, Hugh was delighted by the way the episode
had unfolded and said that it was surely impossible to film a more
bizarre bit of angling. But he was wrong.

On the following evening, Bob found a group of carp feeding
close in beneath a curtain of willow boughs so dense that he
couldn't get a bait through to them. So he climbed up into the
trees and got above them and I went with him, as an arboreal
gillie. I not only took the net, thinking I'd be able to reach down
to enmesh any fish Bob hooked, I took a little device that would
overcome the problem of casting amongst dense branches. As we
were high enough we could see, between gaps in the leaves, several big carp feeding quite confidently and enthusiastically below
us. 'Now how am I going to get a bait to those fish?' asked Bob.

From one hollow handle of the net I revealed the Mark One
blowpipe - a four foot length of $1/4"$ conduit piping. Bob baited his
hook with a bit of moulded superpaste and I dropped this down
the length of the pipe. Then, after asking Bob to open the pick-
up of his reel and point the rod at the fish of his desire, I shot the
bait just a yard beyond target. Bob inched it back into position
and we settled down, slightly precariously, to wait.

We could plainly see that the fish feeding near the bait was a
leather carp and it was truffling in a slow circle, sending up a big
pinkish-coloured cloud of disturbed silt. We were certain it had
no idea it was being fished for but we were still slightly surprised
when, after just a few minutes, the line drew gently taut. Bob
made a firm strike and the carp's lunging response almost had
him head first out of the tree. But then it seemed that we were
going to have to jump out of the tree anyway because after all my
clever ideas about netting from above, we realised we were much
too high.

I don't know if Bob has ever thought of entering the Olympics as a high diver, but after seeing his performance from the top of the willow I think he'd get Britain the gold. Unfortunately, my effort would not have gained many points for style and I came out of the tree like a wounded loris.

The water was deeper than I'd thought and when I'd got myself upright out of the wreckage of a willow branch I found I was standing waist deep. Bob was a few yards from me, rod curving almost dangerously and his reel making interesting noises. The fish had gone straight across the pool towards the willows on the far side and he only just swerved it round at the last moment. We saw a big tail, then a great uprush of white spray and the carp headed up the pool. There were snags and sunken branches all round us, but Bob was too good an angler to allow the fish to make use of them. After a fairly serious argument, the carp realised there was no denying the waiting net and within another minute it was all over and we were admiring another superb-looking 24-pounder. It was the colour of mahogany and it glowed in the late evening sun.

We later discovered, through an old but perfectly defined photograph, that this fish had been caught at almost exactly the same weight 36 years earlier!

We'd got a soaking, we'd risked broken bones, but it was definitely worth it. Hugh agreed, though he said he'd failed to get a really good shot of us jumping out of the tree and suggested that we repeat the stunt. Bob and I just laughed at him.

Later, when we were sitting with dry clothes and a scalding mug of tea, watching the smouldering twilight, Hugh was more encouraging. In fact he was more than simply appreciative of the week in general. He'd travelled the world and filmed in many wonderful places, from the high Andes to the African plains, from the Arctic to the Antarctic (it's just coincidence that these all begin with 'A'). But he said that this jaunt to Redmire was the best trip he'd ever been on.

There was no denying our good fortune: a brace of 20-pounders apiece, and an almost constant celestial smile from Isaak. As the moon came up and the claret replaced the tea, we knew we were going to have to make the entire damn series.

3

Childhood Dreams

Water is peculiar stuff. It circulates mysteriously, rising invisibly from the sea as vapour, forming clouds, falling as rain, creating streams and rivers that return again to the sea. You can swallow it in sips, but it can swallow you whole if you fall into a deep place. You can't catch hold of it, but it can catch hold of you, even if you just look at it.

I was watching my son Alexander the other day, as he stood next to our village pond. He's probably no more excitable and hyperactive than any other frenetic four-year-old, but I sometimes think that his enthusiasm for everything in the world will make him explode. He was happily flicking balls of mud off the end of a stick when a breeze blew, texturing the pond's surface with small ripples. He stopped what he was doing and stood still for the first time in an hour, his eyes fixed on the water as if he'd only just noticed it. Then a cloud slid away from the sun so that the ripples flickered like flames.

Alex seemed to be letting himself become hypnotised (or should that read hydrotised?). But then he laughed and turned to me with a big smile on his face. 'Lovely!' he said.

Any child can get transfixed like that, for there is a universal appeal - an almost magnetic attraction - in water. And once a child has been attracted, it sometimes takes only a momentary glimpse of a fish moving below the surface for something else to happen. The water becomes more than just a strange element - it suddenly becomes another world, more fantastic and compelling than the dry world. It was just a fish, yet it looked so fascinating, so unusual as it appeared from out of the depths. And though it seemed illogical, it became urgently important to try and catch it - as if some secret were bound up in it.

Being the son of an angler, there wasn't much chance of Alexander missing the sight of his first fish. I didn't have to point it out to him and once he'd spotted it - and all the others that swam by afterwards - there was no hope for him. Whether his father was an angler or not was immaterial - all that mattered was that he was going to be an angler. He made his own rod out of a toy golf club with the head removed and last summer he caught a carp of over 1lb! Nothing quite compares with the magic of a boy's first fishing days, when there is more chance of not catching than catching, and when every hour by the waterside is a genuine adventure. Watching Alexander fishing I realise there is very little actual thinking going on in his head and even less dreaming. He is too precariously balanced for such luxuries, sensing himself constantly on the edge of some momentous drama. He is charged with even more dynamism than normal and though he realises he'll probably only catch a tiddler there is never enough time for it all. He is in too much of a hurry to wait for a bite. If his float doesn't move within half a minute he recasts. He continually moves to a 'more better' fishing position. And then, finally, a fish is caught and there will always be, after the usual triumphant shout, a few moments of blissful calm. He stares appreciatively at it, for here is something beautiful that he feels he has almost created himself. Then, gently, as he's been taught, he releases it.

His bristling excitement will, after a year or two, give way to a more reflective, thoughtful approach. And yet, even now, there

OVERLEAF: *The magic of tench fishing: mist, sunrise, lily pads and a well-bent rod*

are times in the midst of his frantic casting when something other than a fish will catch his eye and he'll become still for a while, hypnotised by the ripples again or spellbound by a dragonfly, a pondskater or a whirlygig beetle.

Childhood angling is full of marvels, but of course it is the fish - or the anticipation of the fish - that makes it truly magical. Most fishermen discover their passion for angling in childhood, a time when senses are sharp and magic is authentic, so they all feel nostalgic towards those early days.

We decided to go back to our watery roots to see if we could rediscover those elements that made our boyhood adventures so dramatic, exciting and compelling. It was interesting when we compared our experiences. So many of our inspirational sources were the same: the appearance of a painted float on a still surface, the ring of ripple made by a rising fish, Mr Crabtree, the contents of other angler's keepnets, the smell of a reedy pond in summer, the display of rods and reels in tackle shop windows, the angling section at the local library, a glimpsed shadow looming mysteriously in the depths.

But while we dreamt of monsters we were, during our first casts, more realistic in our expectations. We knew there was more hope of a small roach or perch than a carp or tench. But we would still fish with a wild optimism, even though we'd probably only catch a gudgeon or minnow. Occasionally, something extraodinary would happen, like the time when Bob caught a 1lb roach after cycling to the Thames early one morning before school, or when the miracle of a rudd happened at the end of my line when I was fishing in my village pond.

'In this episode,' said Hugh, 'we'll go back to the sort of places that fired our enthusiasm and see if we can rediscover our earliest angling dreams.' But it is always a dangerous step to go back to places you once held dear and which you haven't visited for years. Many of the ponds I used to fish as a boy have simply vanished - victims of either drought, neglect, tidy-minded farmers, building projects or motorways. And while once-rare species like the king carp are now widespread, the more attainable jewels of our childhood, like rudd and crucian carp, have almost faded from the angling scene altogether.

We decided to return to a water that we knew had not suffered the ravages of time - Frensham Little Pond. Both Bob and I had happy memories of this place from boyhood years. The heathland landscape was virtually unchanged (thanks to the National Trust) and the pond itself, as far as we knew, still held a good number of tench as well as a few big and beautiful rudd. Tench and rudd figured large in our early dreams and so they made the ideal introduction to our new episode.

Returning to this old haunt would also give us the opportunity to see again one of angling's most evocative images - a tench float on a midsummer dawn, before the mist has lifted. It was an image we knew even before we'd experienced its reality as all our favourite angling books described it.

Eventually, the image became a familiar one - but it has never lost its magic. Hugh saw it first in a Fenland dyke, Bob saw it first on the Longwater at Hampton Court and I saw it first at a tench pond near Cobham, Surrey. Now we wanted to see it again at Frensham and not only get it on film, but record its wonderful disappearance.

A great-crested grebe feeding her young

Bob and I fished in the marginal reedbeds along the pond's southern bank, standing about 50 yards apart, waiting for our floats to signal that first faint contact with the depths.

Hugh was also in the reedbeds, with his tripod up to its knees in water, filming a great crested grebe while he waited for the tench.

My float twitched sideways and gracefully sailed away. Tench? No, it was smaller and less muscular. Rudd? No. Roach! I'd never caught a roach at Frensham Little Pond before and this was quite a respectable specimen, over 1lb. I heard a distant splash and turned to see that Bob was also landing a fish. Whether it was a rudd or roach I couldn't tell, but it was obviously no tench. I tried sweetcorn, maggots and breadflake and caught roach almost every cast. Years before, it was rare to catch anything but tench once the fish had found your groundbait and started to feed. You could catch tench all day, but this time, though we fished all day, there wasn't even a sign of one.

After the success of our Redmire visit we'd expected that a classic tench fishing dawn would be an absolute doddle to film. Hugh didn't envisage a lengthy sequence as it was merely intended to evoke the right kind of atmosphere for the scenes that would follow, so we imagined we'd be home for tea. But first the tench proved elusive and then the weather took a dislike to us. We decided to stay on, sleeping on the banks overnight, thinking that the following dawn would at least look the part, but heavy cloud rolled in at first light and it began to rain. It rained for two days and a night. Also, the temperature plummeted. The roach kept biting and we caught a few nice rudd, but we began to suspect that the tench had migrated to another planet.

On the third day, Bob was woken by a strange tapping sound and opened his eyes to the sight of a kingfisher beating a small fish against the butt of his rod. The rod was on rests, and the bird had obviously decided that it was a perfect feeding perch. Suddenly there was a scratching from above as another kingfisher arrived on the scene, landing on the rim of Bob's brolley! The two colourful fisherfowl made Bob's camp their own and though obviously alert and shy they made an easy breakfast for Hugh's camera, which had filmed some of the rarest birds in the world. Bob's dogs, Chester and Rapps, who'd been with us throughout, were so impressed they decided to get in on the act.

ABOVE: *A stunning example of tinca tinca, Bob's Frensham tench of just under 8lbs*

We failed again at sunrise to catch our intended quarry, but Bob caught a wonderful 2lb rudd and what with that and the kingfishers, Hugh decided we had made a good enough start. So we called a temporary tench truce, and as the sun went in again behind stormy clouds, we beat a hasty retreat.

During our time at the Little Pond (a bit of a misnomer, really, as it must be 30 acres) we had various reports from other anglers of the tench fishing at Frensham Great Pond, just a mile away across the heath. It seemed the fish there were under the influence of a more generous god. One evening a friend of ours, Dave Ball, had come over to see how we were doing and share a pot of tea. He'd just had, he said, a very satisfactory haul from the Great Pond, with several fish to just over 6lbs and two over 7lbs. 'They're feeding really well,' he said, 'you should switch venues.'

But besides being more picturesque, the Little Pond was far more peaceful and undisturbed than the Great Pond. The Great Pond was definitely on the beaten track, with an A-road running along the east bank, a massive car park on the north bank (to cater for the huge summer crowds of bathers and paddlers) and a hotel at the south-west corner. It may have been producing the fish, but it lacked the essentially tranquil tench fishing atmosphere. However, the fact that it completely contradicted our idea of classic tench

OPPOSITE: 'My wooden rods, antique reels and old cork-bodied floats would look appropriate at a traditional tench water'

fishing inspired Hugh to rethink our introductory sequence. We could still have the evocative image of the tench float in a still, misty dawn, but we'd contrast it with a different, more unconventional scene.

Because of the weather and the rather depressing lack of traditional tench ponds (what had happened to them all, we wondered?) it took time before we actually found the right location for our original idea. Through the generosity of tackle manufacturer Peter Drennan, we discovered a tench angler's dream.

The ideal tench water should not only be undisturbed, it should have an almost hallowed air, with banks shadowed by ancient trees, its margins thick with reedbeds and its surface studded by lily pads. Peter Drennan's lake not only had all these qualities, it also had an old boathouse and a wonderful punt which, of course, we put to good use. I say 'we' but actually I only mean 'me' because this is where Hugh departed from the original script.

There can be definite advantages to being a narrow-minded purist and pious fundamentalist. My wooden rods, antique reels and old cork-bodied floats would obviously look entirely appropriate at a traditional tench water, while Bob, being gleamingly possessed of all the latest high-tech gear, would not look out of place in a busier, more contemporary angling setting like that at Frensham Great Pond. So while I prepared to punt across a sea of lilies into a mist-veiled sunrise, Bob had the unenviable prospect of having his rods trampled by hordes of bathers and picnickers. Yet, though I felt confident of catching a tench for the camera, it was probably not going to be a particularly large one. Peter told us that there were few, if any, outsize specimens in his lake, while Frensham Great Pond regularly produced great tench. Bob might not find much comfort for the spirit, but he'd almost certainly find another reward.

I moored the punt at the edge of a semi-circular clearing in the lilies and dragged a rake through the swim a couple of times, something all the old traditionalists used to do to stir up the larvae and shrimps in the silt. It seemed a dubious act because of the rake's clumping splash, but it was obviously effective, for the ripples from it had only just subsided when a cluster of small, fish-generated bubbles appeared like stars on the dark surface. The tench had apparently been attracted and were now beginning to browse over the freshly-ploughed lake bed. I baited with a goodly-sized chunk of luncheon meat and set the float so that the bait lay well on the bottom, in about six feet of water. It was a nice-looking float, olive green and yellow with a red tip, and it looked even more attractive when it was sitting, cocked, by the lilies, completing a scene that seemed to have been created for it.

Another peppering of bubbles appeared and then, a minute later, the float slowly disappeared and there followed that wonderful momentary interval when there is nothing to see but everything to expect. I struck and knew as soon as the rod curved over that this was no roach or rudd. I could feel the throb of a broad paddle-like tail as the fish drove towards the lily stems and only a tench could make the line pulsate like that. As the hole in the lilies was only about 12-feet across it was quite a tight tussle in the confined space. The fish wasn't a big one, but it fought with that dogged tenaciousness that is typical of all tench, especially the males. Eventually, I eased a plump 3-pounder over the net, the same kind of size as the ones I used to catch in boyhood. Its glossy flanks were bullrush green, the undersides primrose yellow and the little gold eye was rimmed with red.

The sun rose higher above the thin transparent mist, the dawn chorus trailed away to near silence, a carp rolled in open water and spread a slow circle of ripple from bank to bank.

I re-baited and recast and the float settled again, pert and expectant, on the edge of the lilies. Less pert, but just as expectant, I settled back in the punt and waited for another bite...

Bob's world was over a million miles away. Instead of birdsong he had a chorus of transistor radios; instead of moorhens and dabchicks in his swim he had bathers with beach balls and small boys on lilos. After the serenity of 'Lake Drennan' it was like the third circle of hell, yet Bob (and his faithful dogs) emerged from it gloriously. He could have fished further away from the revellers, but he made the astute point that they acted like a giant rake, continually stirring up the bottom and therefore attracting rather than disturbing the tench. Obviously he kept to the edge of the splashing throng, but he cast his baits so that any fish entering the area from the eastern bank couldn't fail to find them.

His theory paid off because, in the middle of a blazing hot afternoon, two really beautiful creatures surfaced in his swim.

Both were female, one being the usual homo sapiens, but red-headed and wearing a stunning black bikini, and the other was an amazing example of tinca tinca, the tench, weighing just under 8lbs. Luckily, he missed the former on the strike, but then his bite indicator had sounded again above the general hubub and he hooked the latter.

The pond was comparatively shallow, so the fish made a series of quite long, powerful runs before coming between a pack of waterbabies towards the net. Eventually it rolled on its side and Bob coaxed it over the mesh - the biggest tench he'd ever caught (and over twice the size of my fish!)

Most of our childhood was spent paddling round stillwaters. But rivers and streams flowed strongly through our formative years, especially those small, clear rivers where you could look down through the depths and perhaps see a monster. Therefore, as we wanted to capture all the images from boyhood, we had a perfect excuse for a refreshing change of scene. We would visit a fast-flowing river, and indulge in barbel fishing.

We chose the Hampshire Avon above Downton, where the river runs virtually past Bob's back garden, and we had another one of our little challenges - best barbel wins a pint of beer. And like the Little Pond scenario, this was only envisaged as a short sequence - a brief interval between more substantive episodes. However, the best laid plans...

There was a shoal of quite large barbel inhabiting a deep pool above an iron bridge and it was there that I chose to fish. Though I could occasionally see the fish - and it was a sight that would have driven me crazy when I was a lad - it was soon apparent that they didn't seem to understand the meaning of sweetcorn or luncheon meat or even maggots. On my first attempt at the shoal I didn't get a bite and Hugh didn't shoot any film.

Bob made a wiser choice and settled down to fish a swim where he knew, from previous experience, that the barbel were familiar with his baits. And on his first attempt, with Hugh standing by, he managed two fish: a small chub and an eel. We had a good dose of rain the next day and what with a gently rising river and a few buckets of groundbait, we were horribly confident of success. My deep pool, above a bend and surrounded by dense

OPPOSITE: *'When we were young we used to spend hours gazing down into water, either watching the shadowy movements of fish or imagining we were watching them'*

beds of water buttercup, looked even more promising than before and I said that Hugh should get himself immediately in focus, 'because I'm going to get one first cast!'

The extra current necessitated a half ounce leger to keep my bait - luncheon meat - firmly on the gravel bottom. I could then inch it down the length of the pool with more control than if I'd used a lighter lead. But nothing grabbed it and I turned with on apologetic expression to Hugh, who just smiled and raised his eyebrows, as if to say, surely you weren't really expecting anything? But I was, I was!

The second cast dropped the bait in exactly the same spot as before and this time, halfway down the pool, there was a quick jag followed by a decisive heave and I struck into a good fish.

'Barbel!' I said, as something deep and powerful made a slow irresistible plunge into the weedbeds. My nicely-tapered barbel rod - specially made for me by master cane-splitter, Edward Barder - went into a critical bend and I thought, 'Blimey, this is going to be some fish!' It would have made a very acceptable barbel, but unfortunately it turned out to be a 10lb carp, the first and only carp I've ever caught in the Avon.

As carp were part of my original childhood dream, I'll always hold them in high esteem, but I prefer them in their customary stillwater homes and not in a quick-flowing barbel swim. I fished on, but I didn't get another bite, even though it was a perfect evening for barbel.

Hugh went the half-mile upstream to see how Bob was faring. He was casting into a gully on the outside of a bend, where the bank was overhung by alders and the river was wide and evenly flowing. Hugh didn't have long to wait before Bob's sweetcorn was confidently snaffled and a big fish took off downstream. Patiently and carefully, Bob worked it back towards the waiting net. There was a fierce splash and plunge as he drew it between the arms. He lifted, and there it was on the bank - another carp!

Bob and I have made a habit of duplicating catches like this. Harmonic convergence, we call it, but our first filmed barbel expedition was the wrong time to continue the phenomenon.

Bob tossed in some more hempseed groundbait, re-baited with Pepperami instead of corn and just before the light became too low for filming, hooked another fish. This one ran upstream

OVERLEAF: *'With my silken line and slender hook I wander in a myriad of ripples and find - freedom'*

and kept to a slower, more stubbornly fixed course. Surely it had to be a barbel. It speared itself into a small but thick weedbed and became unbudgable, so Bob pushed his way down the overgrown bank to alter the direction of pull. The fish was dislodged and after another minute he had it wallowing over the mesh. A

very welcome and fine-fettled barbel of over 7lbs. It was, therefore, I who bought the beer that night, even though it was Bob
who had to lend me the fiver for the round.

When we were young, we used to spend hours - days - hanging
over a grassy bank or lying along a willow bough gazing down into
the water, either watching the shadowy movements of fish or
imagining we were watching them. When a larger-than-average
shape ghosted into view - say a big chub or a pike - it seemed as if
the air around us almost crackled with tension. And the fact that
the monsters seemed completely unattainable only deepened
their mystery.

This was another little scene, familiar to most anglers - ordinary, yet indescribably compelling - that we wanted to recreate:
we would find a group a big fish somewhere along the river where
Hugh could film them, then introduce a fisher-boy to them and
see if his eyes popped out. Sometime during early August, Bob
found a shoal of barbel and chub down at a very picturesque spot
known as Barford Island. He walked down there from his house
and fished it for an entire day, landing several chub, half a dozen
barbel and hooking and losing a monster that looked over 12lbs.
Though the pool was quite deep it was possible to see the fish
when the sun was directly overhead and there were also shallows
above and below giving more potential for filming.

When he went back next time, Bob had both Hugh and me
following behind. It certainly looked a delectable spot and as Bob
set up his rods we could see a great swathe of chub dappling the
riverbed with shadows. But we couldn't then see any barbel. I
went off upstream, looking for other signs, and came to a place
where a narrow gravel run shelved down alongside an overhanging bank, dropping eventually into a deep, dark pool. Because of
a dense midstream weedbed, the current accelerated over the
gravel, but as we were in the middle of another summer drought
it wasn't exactly a rush of water. In fact algae was establishing
itself over the gravel, turning the gold to a dull brown. Though it
looked an ideal spot, there was nothing visible within it. I was just
about to go when I glimpsed a movement out of the corner of my
eye and turned back to see a barbel drifting out of the weedbeds
and slowly dropping downstream.

Where there is one barbel, there are often others, so I sprinkled the gravel with hempseed and sweetcorn and went on upstream. Half an hour later, having found only a few small chub and dace, I came back and there, right under the bank, was a shoal of a dozen barbel, all feeding on the groundbait. They ranged from about 5-10lbs and as they slowly worked upstream into shallower water they became more and more clearly visible, boldly writing themselves into the script.

As it was school summer holidays, we had no shortage of

A SIMPLE APPROACH TO THE MYSTERIOUS BARBEL

Angling methods - especially nowadays - can be confusingly sophisticated and complicated. My barbel tackle is old and Bob's modern, but in our view it is always advisable to err on the side of simplicity.

My own barbel tackle could not be more basic: rod, centrepin reel, box of hooks, a few swan shot and bait. The fishing technique is equally simple, with the tackle weighted just enough for the bait to 'trundle' enticingly through the barbel's lair, or per-

haps be checked so that it lies tantalisingly and semi-stationary in front of its whiskery nose.

While delicate bites need a practised eye or hand to detect, there is no mistaking a hungry barbel's savage snatch. The only demanding aspect of this technique is in the specialised type of cast - the Wallis cast - if great distance is required. But most anglers can master this cast in time. And if they can't, they can always revert to the fixed-spool reel. However, the real secret of success lies not in how you cast but where.

young fisherfolk willing to help with our sequence. Naturally, we needed someone without too much angling experience or the whole point of the exercise - the surprise factor - would be lost. When I'd been fish-spotting upstream I'd seen a local lad, Peter Hugo, fishing for minnows at the tail of a weirpool. He was exactly right for our part, looking like a latter-day Huckleberry Finn, with a bamboo pole for a rod and a length of string knotted to the end. I hoped he'd be using a bent pin and was rather disappointed, when Hugh and I went up to speak to him, to find a new size 14 to nylon neatly hitched to the end of the string.

Just as we used to do as children, Peter was temporarily keeping his catch in a jam jar and one of his minnows was the biggest I'd ever seen - well over an ounce! Yet despite the minnows' eagerness for his baits, he was quite happy to abandon them for a while as he said he'd never seen a barbel before. He wasn't bothered about the camera either, in fact when we reached my swim and cautiously peered over the bankside vegetation into the clear depths, he forgot about it altogether. 'Wow!' he said. He was genuinely amazed. We were very lucky. The spot where we'd got the barbel to feed was one of only a few such places along the entire length of the Avon. It was ideal for light, perfect for depth and most importantly, it hadn't been fished for years. It enabled Hugh to film Peter and the barbel simultaneously. Moreover, Hugh could focus right down through the transparent depths and pick out the detail of individual specimens.

Just watching the barbel, however, could not ultimately be as exciting as actually fishing for them and Peter was obviously dying to have a cast. It would've been nice to have seen how he got on with his own gear, but I offered him my own bamboo pole which was, after all, specially whittled for barbel and even had an old reel attached.

I cast out with the simplest of tackle, a size 8 baited with sweetcorn and two swan shot on the line, and then gave the rod to Peter. It seemed certain that we'd get a bite almost immediately as the fish were still feeding enthusiastically over the groundbait. They were actually clearing away the film of algae, effectively polishing the gravel, yet an hour passed and, despite recasts and bait changes, nothing responded to our efforts. Peter wasn't disappointed or even surprised. After all, it was enough just to have seen such wondrous creatures. Surely it was only in myth that

Another boyhood dream comes true: Peter with his first barbel which weighed 8lbs 6oz

they were ever caught. There was always a chance, though, I said and he was obviously still quite tense with anticipation, hoping he was about to catch the biggest fish of his life.

As we talked, a kingfisher flew upstream and landed on the rod. Now I realise that when we were tench fishing, Bob, the true specimen hunter, had two kingfishers on his rod, but it was still something that had only happened to me once before in 30 years of angling. Hugh caught the moment perfectly and was even able to zoom in slowly between Peter and myself to a sharply beaked profile. Yet despite that lucky turquoise streak, we still failed to catch a barbel. Though keen on the free offerings, the shoal had carefully avoided every hook bait we tried.

We packed up at sunset and were just setting off along the bank when we heard the rasp of Bob's reel. 'Maybe you'll see a barbel after all,' I said as we broke into a run towards Barford Island. With his curved rod nicely silhouetted against the after-glow, Bob was leading a fish down to the tail of the deep pool. 'Is

'As we talked a king-fisher flew upstream and landed on the rod'

it a barbel?' asked Peter, breathlessly. 'No,' replied Bob, 'it's a chub.' Not a bad one, though, and I slipped the net under a portly three-pounder.

Bob had seen a couple of really large barbel in his swim and had hoped, as the daylight faded, that they'd begin to feed. Therefore the chub was a bit of an anti-climax. We couldn't complain, though. It had been a near-perfect summer day on the river and the perfect way to end it was in the local pub. Tomorrow, we said, we'd be back again, and if Peter wished he could have another try for a barbel.

Naturally, Peter was there early next morning and - much to our delight - so were the barbel. This time I let Peter swing the bait into the swim and it had only just settled when I actually saw a fish turn for it and take it. The line tightened, the rod tip quivered over and almost before he'd realised it, our Huckleberry had hooked a barbel.

It raced off downstream, pulling Peter after it and making me shout to remind him that now he'd got a reel, he could let the fish have as much line as it wanted. The barbel went down into the main pool, luckily avoiding the weedbeds, and then made a fierce rush right across the river. The rod was slammed down to the horizontal and Peter had his knuckles rapped as, luckily, the reel handle was torn from his grip. If he'd held tighter, the line would have snapped like cotton.

It was a powerful fish, but after that tremendous lunge, Peter began to master the concept of the centre-pin reel and get a measure of control. Within a few minutes, we saw a graceful gold form rising towards the surface. Of course I'd left the net up the bank and had to go racing back for it but Peter hung on, even though the whole situation had rendered him almost speechless. He let the fish have line when it dived, reeled in gently when it allowed, and after I'd clambered down the bank onto a reedy tussock, he led it carefully and steadily over the net.

Then we cheered and laughed as I lifted out a beautiful, golden eight-pounder, and Peter's beaming, slightly incredulous expression showed that another boyhood dream had come true.

4

In Search of Salmon

ABOVE: *Rapps, our brilliant canine gillie, demonstrating his unique talent*

LEFT: *'The Spey was low and clear'*

When we originally discussed with Hugh the making of a television series, Bob and I didn't envisage spending much time in the company of trout or salmon. Though we often enjoy game fishing, and though Bob is a brilliant fly caster, we much prefer the kinds of game played by the so-called 'coarse' fish. If you compare strength alone, there is not much to choose between a salmon and a carp, but in animal intelligence the difference is vast. A carp has the largest brain of all our freshwater fish and the salmon has, proportionately, one of the smallest. Taking on a big wild carp is like challenging a chess grandmaster. The salmon, on the other hand, is certainly a game fish but, like a video game, it will only play if it is switched on, and if the water is not right you may as well go home. Trout - brown trout that is - can be highly demanding and rewarding, but not, in our

'We'd not gone far when we saw a movement in the foliage - it was a roe deer'

view, as demanding or rewarding as a really big roach or chub.

We, naturally, had far more to say about the species of fish we had grown up with; and we were familiar with the infinite variety of waters associated with them. In fact there were so many possibilities bound up in just a few favourite species that we could have made double the number of programmes and still not explored all their potential. So surely there wouldn't be enough space or time for trout and salmon?

Unfortunately, Hugh heard about Bob's dog.

At that time, Bob had two delightful and intelligent flat-coated retrievers, Chester and Rapps. They were astonishingly well-trained and obedient, but Bob, who used to work them on shooting estates, had taught them that it wasn't only pheasants and partridges that required their attention. A weeded fish could present a problem that only a retriever could solve.

Rapps, the elder of the pair, had made such a speciality of landing trout, weeded or not, that when he accompanied his master to the river at mayfly time there was never need of a net. Hugh obviously felt that these canine antics would make an entertaining introduction to a day's trout fishing.

So, on a fine summer morning we duly assembled at a well-stocked beat of the Avon and waited for the trout to rise. When I arrived, Bob was already in midstream, casting his Grey Duster up into a shallow glide alongside a line of willows. The fish had been active but non-compliant and Rapps was looking slightly bored, sitting in the shade of a tree and no doubt longing for a swim. Like Hugh, I had not actually seen this gillie in action, so when Bob finally hooked a good trout, I found myself wondering whether the performance would come up to expectations. I needn't have worried. Rapps came and sat quietly at the river's edge until the fish was played out and lying on its side. Then, on a word from Bob, he plunged into the water and took the trout from the surface as neatly as if it had been a dog biscuit. He and Bob splashed ashore and Rapps carefully placed the fish in his master's hand. It was a beautifully coloured brownie of about 1½lbs and Rapps, the true professional, had not damaged or dislodged even a single scale. To emphasise the point, Bob slipped the fish back and it shot away with an energetic tail swipe.

Hugh was enormously impressed and got the whole performance on film. But I got carried away and said something daft. 'Do you think Rapps could do that with a salmon?' It was a question I immediately regretted. I'd been nursing this happy idea that I could spend the programme contentedly stalking chub while Bob demonstrated the art of trout fishing. However, with Hugh suddenly enthusing about Rapps and a salmon, my secret plan went west and we all headed north - to Bonnie Scotland.

I have caught plenty of salmon on spinners and worms - and other things - but I've never actually caught one on a fly and I don't think Bob has 'done it properly' more than twice. So before trying our luck on our chosen river, the Spey, we decided to break our journey and perhaps pick up a few tips on the Tweed. We had a couple of friends, David and Kim Louis Stewart, fishing the famous Floors Castle stretch. The salmon were running and David and Kim, both expert flyfishers, could give us some valuable instruction. Bob accompanied David, who is a keen if reckless

OVERLEAF: *Arrival at the Spey. Bob and I were astonished by the beauty of the place. We were eager to wet our lines, the dogs were desperate to jump in*

81

wader, while I had the pleasure of a boat trip with Kim. David began fishing the inside of a long sweeping bend and, with Hugh filming from the bank, he hooked a salmon after only ten minutes. However, just as he began applying some pressure, it jagged the hook free and with a heavy swirl, sped off downstream. Bob and Hugh offered condolences: but with other fish leaping enthusiastically, and the river in perfect order after rain, David told them there would be plenty more chances.

Kim was just as optimistic and, perhaps even more encouraging, so was Peter, Kim's gillie. Peter looked upon that stretch of river as if it were a familiar face and he could accurately judge its moods according to its changes of expression. Today it was undoubtedly looking generous. He effortlessly guided our boat alongside the head of a deep pool and Kim cast a diagonal line across and down, allowing her fly - a Gordon's Fancy - to swing round in the fast current. After just four casts Kim's line drew suddenly taut, making an audible hiss as it cut through the surface and her rod top swooped over. Almost imperceptibly, Peter began to row the boat into quieter, shallower water.

The salmon kept deep and slow to begin with but, with Kim holding it extremely firmly and not allowing it to build up any momentum, it finally broke surface with a shower of spray. There were a couple of short, heavy rushes downstream, then Kim began to regain line. Peter, who throughout the battle had been carefully working the boat into quieter, shallower water, now stowed the oars, picked up the landing net and stepped into the river. Then, while keeping the boat stationary in the current at the same time, he waited until Kim steered the fish past him. Peter leaned suddenly forward, there was an explosion in the mesh and almost before we knew it we had our first salmon, a bright cock fish of about 15lbs.

I was impressed. Kim made it look so easy. She gave wonderful credence to the long-held theory about women being better salmon anglers than men - a theory recently, if rather dubiously, explained by the quality of female pheromones. If true this could prove to be a sap to my confidence because, however much I improve my fly casting (and it does need a bit of improvement), I can't do anything about my pheromones.

We dropped down the pool and Kim began casting again. We discussed another theory: my belief that fish can sometimes

detect an angler's concentration and will only take when that concentration lifts. If Kim and I stopped thinking about the fish we
might catch another one. The slight downstream bow in Kim's
line pulled rapidly straight and the reel rasped. Another salmon,
another good one and a nice example of my theory.

'There we are,' I said, 'we switched our minds off.'

'I didn't,' laughed Kim.

*'We saw a salmon rise
up in the foam and then
disappear'*

The fish pulled even harder than the first and Kim reacted by putting even more of a hoop into her 14-foot rod: it was quite a dramatic sight. Once more, Peter gently guided the boat into some quiet shallows. Having spotted the flurry of activity, Hugh arrived on the scene and was able to wade right out to us with the camera on his shoulder. I got into the water as well so that I could hold the boat steady and give Peter more net room.

There was a flash of silver as the salmon turned near the surface, then it swept powerfully away upstream, swinging the rod point round after it. Kim let it have its head for a while, then checked it firmly and it came round in a wide circle. We all agreed that it was a big fish and there were murmers of appreciation as it cruised past us, plainly visible in the sunlit water. Within a few moments, Kim had turned it again and as it made another, slower pass, Peter carefully waded forward. With a quick, accurate thrust, the net went in, there was an abrupt explosion of water and so another salmon was hammocked in the mesh: a gleaming fresh-run fish of exactly 20lbs.

In just two days, Kim and David caught almost two dozen salmon and, suitably inspired, Bob, Hugh and I headed north again for the Spey. We were going to fish a stretch just south of Aviemore, where the river winds through thickly wooded country in the shadow of two great mountain ranges - the Cairngorms and the Monadhliaths. Hugh knew the area intimately as it had been the location for several of his most successful wildlife films. It was the classic hunting country of osprey, golden eagle, goshawk and peregrine falcon, and the wild tree-bordered river provided the perfect environment for otters.

Hugh described all the scenery and the wildlife graphically as we neared our destination, but both Bob and I were still astonished by the beauty of the place when we saw it. Chester and Rapps, who had been on the leash at Floors Castle, thought it was paradise.

However, the rains that had benefited the Tweed had not done much for the Spey and the river was low and clear. Though we fished our way through several exquisite-looking pools along two miles of bank, we didn't see a sign of a salmon. Eventually Bob made a determined effort to catch a seatrout, having discovered a superb, deep glide below a very fast narrow run. Understanding the habits of this other 'silver tourist', he felt he'd

found the text-book holding pool. But first he caught one of the native brownies - admittedly a lovely fish of over 2lbs - and then he hooked something much heavier which turned out to be a large and very ancient horseshoe.

'Surely a sign from Isaak!' he said. I had a sign from Isaak as well. As I fished a big, swirling eddy something rose up and broke the surface right under my rod tip. The sun had just set and the light wasn't good enough for me to see instantly what the creature was. But then it turned and blinked at me. It was an otter! I could have tickled its nose with the rod. It was only there for perhaps two or three seconds, then it dived with a big splash and both Bob and Hugh, just upstream of me, thought I'd hooked a fish.

I did hook a fish a few minutes later. Something grabbed my

One of our regular lunchtime siestas by the Spey

size 4 Willy Gunn and I reeled in a half-pound rainbow trout!

Hugh had an old caravan permanently parked in a birch wood near the river and we used this as base camp for over a fortnight as we vainly flogged the water and hoped for a salmon. But if we began showing signs of frustration, Chester and Rapps were not in the least bothered by the lack of drama. They were always happy to savour the wondrous scents of badger, hare, red squirrel and rabbit around the caravan and they could exult in the heavenly pong of otter spraints along the riverbank. There was also the powerful fishy aroma to be enjoyed under a local osprey's plucking post. And whenever Rapps (the younger and more energetic of the pair) fancied a swim, Bob would oblige by going trout fishing and asking him to land a few brownies.

After one of our usual lunchtime siestas by the riverside, we all went on an otter quest trying to find the local holt. Twice we had seen otters in the late evening and, as they are very much part of the Spey valley, as well as being the most beautiful mammals in Britain, we thought it would be nice if we could get one on film.

We found a spraint (the droppings that mark out an otter's territory) where a little backwater joined the main river. The sidestream was overhung with alders, dark and secluded - just the sort of place that an otter would call home. So we plunged into the shadows, following the stream, to see where it led. We'd not gone far when we saw a movement through the foliage, but it was only a roe deer - a very handsome specimen all the same. Then we saw another - the female half of the pair.

After a while, the trees began to thin out and we came upon a wide, shallow lily-covered lake - the stream's source. It looked the perfect habitat for pike and eels and would, we suspected, be a favourite hunting place for hungry herons, osprey and, of course, otters.

And so it proved, for right in the lake's margin, barging through the lilies and looking like playful seals, were not one but three otters. It was a mother and two cubs and they put on a wonderful performance for Hugh's camera. They somersaulted, chased each other's tails, and even smiled into the lens.

Naturally, Bob and I slipped back there on several subsequent occasions with our own cameras, but - surprise, surprise - we weren't as successful as Hugh.

ABOVE: *The treasure of Floors Castle*

RIGHT: *The Dulnain in spate: 'The water was thrashing over the rocks as brown and frothy as beer'*

One day we took the Land Rover and drove out of the Spey valley into the Monadhliath mountains. Hugh wanted to have a look at the Dulnain, a spate river and tributary of the Spey, which might have provided a few fish had there been some water in it. But there was barely a trickle between pools and all the river's bones were showing - the long grooves and ridges in the rocky bed, the dry shelves of shingle, the great boulders, smoothed and sculpted by winter spates. We could imagine, though, how it must have looked when the water was rushing and foaming from the mountain tops and when the silver tourists came rushing and sparkling up to the very end of their long journey.

There was nothing now in the river but, as we gave up looking for fish, we were granted a sight that must surely be unique in Britain, if not the rest of Europe. We had just seen a stoat emerging from the heather to chase a mountain hare when Hugh spotted a goshawk circling over a distant wood. As we watched it, Bob

noticed another more distant movement - three golden eagles soaring along the edge of a mountain ridge. We all focused our binoculars on them and Hugh immediately saw that one of the trio had broader wings and a shorter tail than the other two.

'It's a sea eagle!' said Hugh. 'It must have flown into the others' territory and now they're trying to drive it away.' Of course Hugh was familiar with all these raptors but until that day Bob and I had seen neither species of eagle before and had only rarely glimpsed a goshawk. To have seen them all in the air at the same moment, however, was like seeing a squadron made up of a UFO, a witch on a broomstick and Father Christmas.

The trip was a success as far as bird spotting was concerned, and though Hugh was very pleased with the wildlife sequences he'd managed to shoot, we had to admit defeat on the fishing front. We'd caught plenty of brownies and had seen a few leaping seatrout. Bob and I both managed to hook a salmon, but we were unfortunately trout fishing at one time and our light lines were no match for a champion tackle-smasher.

We would just have to come back again in the autumn, and pray for rain.

The salmon season ended on 30 September and by the middle of that month there had still been no appreciable rainfall. According to reports, a great mass of salmon and seatrout were holding up, down near the mouth of the Spey, waiting for the levels to rise. If the drought didn't end until October there'd be no point in heading north again and we might have to think of an alternative ending to our film - perhaps a spot of lamprey fishing.

Hugh was all prepared for a sudden departure, though, as he was confident the weather would change in time. Bob hoped that it would either change very soon or not at all as his birthday is at the end of September and he always likes to celebrate it by catching a roach. But when it was not quite too late the rains finally returned with a vengeance. Most of the main Scottish rivers rose several feet overnight and as they began to rush, roar and then thunder towards the sea, so the silver tourists began to surge upstream. Bob had to forget about roach and we all had to go salmon fishing on his birthday. Life can be very hard at times.

Rather than fish the Spey, which was running the colour of cement, we decided to try the Dulnain which was only the colour of tea. Also, because our fishing was at the very top of that river,

all the migrants would be reaching their destination right under our rod tips. But best of all, because the Dulnain ran through narrow, rocky canyons, with gushing waterfalls and sudden deep pools, we could revert to what we were best at: we could dispense with our salmon fly rods and fish the worm.

High up in the mountains, at the very head of the river, was a little stone bothy which would become our home for the few remaining days of the season. It was a bit cramped and cave-like, but it provided adequate shelter from the wind and rain; in fact, once we'd got the log fire going, and put the blackened kettle in the flames, it was positively cosy. Apart from the kettle and a pan, though, our fishing lodge lacked any other cooking facilities. Therefore, most meals were preceded by a drive through cloud in the landrover to the nearest four-star restaurant - Hugh's luxury camper, parked halfway down a precipitous mountain track. Hugh had only recently acquired this supply waggon, but it was to prove a tremendous investment on that, and all subsequent location trips. As well as having a built-in fridge, running water, stereo radio - permanently tuned to Radio 3 - and ample storage space, it was also the only vehicle in the country with its own wine cellar.

By the time we'd got ourselves properly established on that first day, it was too late for any serious fishing or filming. In any case, Hugh, mindful of the roach which weren't being caught, said he couldn't possibly ask us to work on Bob's birthday. We did, however, take a short stroll along the river in the evening light and both Hugh and I insisted Bob should bring his rod and have a few casts.

The water was thrashing over the rocks, as brown and frothy as beer. We saw a fish rise up in the foam and then disappear. Bob had a couple of casts for it, but there was no response. At a quieter, deeper pool, his worm was surreptitiously taken, as if by a little trout, but his strike had us all exclaiming, 'It's a salmon!'

Something large and powerful began to circle slowly belowing the arching rod, too deep to see and too obstinate to raise. Chester and Rapps, who had previously been far too interested in the mountain hares to bother about fishing, suddenly looked keenly at the water and I quickly set up the big landing net, in case the situation got out of paw.

Bob wound in and began to apply a more persuasive pressure, but all that happened was that the rod went abruptly straight.

PRECEDING PAGE:
Desperately seeking
salmon: Chris vainly
hoping for some low-
water luck on the Spey

The hook had pulled free. The dogs stared down into the pool as if they didn't quite believe what had happened.

'It got off,'said Bob ruefully, 'because it wasn't a roach.'

Then the clouds descended and it began to rain again so, instead of celebrating Bob's 42nd with a salmon, we hurried back to the bothy. The fire was still glowing in the grate and there were two unopened bottles on the floor - one containing whisky, the other, vintage port.

I woke next morning, surprisingly clear-headed, to the distant cry of pink-footed geese. It was still grey, but the cloud had lifted a good deal in the night, and the rain had slackened to a thin

THE STRANGE ALLURE OF A RAT-FACED MACDOUGAL

Thunder and Lightning, Silver Doctor, Gordon's Fancy (pictured left), Willy Gunn (right), Jock Scott, Birtwhistle's Shrimp, Bulldog, Beauly Snow, Dunkeld, Black Dose... The wonderfully colourful names of salmon flies work like a magical incantation on the salmon fisher, transporting him instantly to the specific place along a river that he associates with a favourite pattern.

And while many successful anglers will have a persuasive argument regarding the choice of fly for certain river conditions, many others will have a less reasoned, more instinctive method of choosing, while others again may be influenced solely by the appeal of those names - Dusty Miller, Logie, Blue Charm, Hairy Mary, General Practitioner, Durham Ranger, Rat-faced MacDougal...

drizzle. I boiled the kettle for tea, made a pan full of porridge, and we breakfasted by the single, cobwebbed window, looking out at the lively river and agreeing that it had come up another six inches in the night. Then Hugh prepared his camera and sound gear, while Bob and I readied our tackle and loaded it all in the back of the landrover.

We drove down to where the Dulnain dived between steep rock walls, where there were several very deep pots and pools connected by falls and fast runs. Walking over to a heathery, boulder-strewn bluff, we had a good view along half a mile of riotous river and, even as we watched, we saw salmon leaping - one, two, three - out of the pool below us, like homing pigeons flying out of a basket.

We clambered down into the rocky gorge, making sure Chester and Rapps didn't topple down the last sheer face, and then, having reached the river, picked our way across stones and boulders until we arrived at the main pool. It was deep and swirling, a cupped storm of bubbles and turbulence, with a ten-foot column of water gushing down from the pool above. A salmon launched itself rocket-like up the fall, reached almost to the top and then fell back with a mighty splash. It seemed we might get a fish after all.

Suddenly we became quite excited. The pool was obviously full of silver tourists, stacking up below the fall; it was also likely to be holding one or two quite large fish and judging by previous experience, we were certain they would grab the first worm they saw.

As we began to tackle up we were further heartened by a break in the clouds and then suddenly, the rain stopped altogether. Bob used a 12-foot carbon barbel rod, Swallow centrepin and 8lb breaking strain line, while I used my 11¾-foot split cane barbel rod, with an old Aerial and, likewise, 8lb line. Next to the camera and tripod stood another rod and reel. All we needed was one salmon 'in the can' and then Hugh could stop work and join us in the fray.

Bob hooked a fish first cast. There was a little jag on the end of his rod and the next second something was trying to drag him into the river. Rapps and Chester became terribly enthusiastic, wanting to jump in straightaway, but Bob told them to behave and they sat obediently, watching the drama with wide eyes.

However, with the salmon charging unstoppably across the pool, and with all the upswirls and vortices we realised it was unwise to let even a semi-amphibious creature like Rapps into the pool. Perhaps later, Bob told him, at a quieter bit of river. Rapps looked at him in despair. And then the despair turned to utter desolation as the salmon slipped the hook.

I missed a nabbing sort of bite, recast nearer the fall and hooked a fish before the bait had touched the bottom. It put a lovely bend in the cane and my thumb became quite hot when it tried to brake the blurring reel. There's no denying that salmon pull incredibly hard, but we finally got that one into the net, a fish of around seven pounds. Unfortunately it had obviously been in the river for some time and had lost most of its lustre. More red rover than silver tourist.

As soon as I'd slipped the salmon back, Hugh grabbed his rod and cast, hooking a fish within minutes. It burst up through the surface, swooped down again and rocketed out of the pool, with Hugh in pursuit. He got it, eventually, a bright 5lb seatrout. Then Bob hooked another salmon and much to the dogs' delight, he was soon able to hold it under their noses for a proper canine inspection. Then both he and I landed a seatrout while Hugh was playing a salmon. It was just luck that we didn't start knitting with our lines. And so it went on, gloriously, fish after fish, and nothing distracted us or interrupted our casting until sunset when, suddenly, a golden eagle appeared, gliding down the length of the valley and giving Hugh plenty of time to train the camera on it. As he filmed it I recast and, after a short wait, hooked the best salmon of the day.

For five minutes the fish was content to circle deeply and slowly in front of us and seemed hardly aware of me at all. Then it swept majestically out of the pool and I raced after it, skidding on wet rocks, sloshing through shallows, jumping boulders. Bob followed with the net and, amazingly, Hugh managed to follow with the camera. The dogs scampered along behind, obviously hoping for some quieter water. Every time I tried to pilot the salmon between rocks and coax it towards our bank it just put on another surge of power and eventually with the reel screeching wonderfully, it dived over the next fall and into the last pool of our beat.

There was a deep gully down the pool's centre and the fish

sank down into it, giving me time to catch up and bring some serious pressure to bear. It made no difference to begin with, but after a while the salmon began to rise and we saw it clearly for the first and last time - a big fish that probably seemed bigger than it was in the dark confines of the gorge. Then there was a sudden horrible adieu. The salmon vanished into the depths and the hook and lead flicked back over our heads.

Rapps and Chester looked from the water into my face and their combined expressions told me that I would never make a proper salmon angler.

Even the redstarts seemed to be mocking my misfortune

5

Autumn Glory

LEFT: *A magnificent autumn barbel from the Hampshire Avon, just upstream from Bob's kitchen*

It was a pleasure to get back to a river that wouldn't shrink and vanish at the first sign of a drought and whose inhabitants remained more or less at home all year round. We were going to spend the autumn on England's most famous angling river, the Hampshire Avon, and fish for those species that reached the peak of their condition when the leaves begin to fall: perch, chub, roach and barbel.

Besides the good fishing, autumn on the Avon is always a happy experience. The valley smoulders with ambers, russets and golds, while the river runs more strongly and more exuberantly than in the summer. Autumn migrants funnel along the southern-flowing course - swallows, martins, swifts and occasionally hobbys and ospreys, together with all the other departing summer visitors, so that you feel a sort of yearning - an ancestral urge - to follow them. But then you look again at the river and think of all those wondrous fish, like fruits at harvest time, and you know you'd be mad to wish yourself anywhere else. It was the Avon in autumn that finally persuaded me to move house from a stillwater paradise on the Surrey-Hampshire border and, as I explained earlier, it was the Avon that lured Bob down from London - a move he'll never regret. But while Bob has been fishing the river for nearly 30 years, I didn't have my first cast into it until 1982. My favourite stretches were just above and below Ringwood - prime barbel water - while Bob spent more time above Fordingbridge, fishing for big roach. So where, precisely, should we make our autumn film?

Hugh has been living and fishing in the area since the mid-seventies and his favourite stretch of river was above Downton, where we filmed in the summer, and where he had already made a superbly evocative film about a year on the Avon, Tom's River.

It was a famous stretch for roach, Hugh's chosen species. There were great shoals of chub and dace, and though the barbel fishing wasn't as good as in the river's lower reaches, there were undoubtedly scattered groups of very large specimens. But, most persuasively of all, the stretch was adjacent to Bob's kitchen with its unlimited supply of exquisite leaf teas. Therefore it was unanimously decided to spend the autumn on the upper river.

Hugh thought it best to begin quietly and not too ambitiously with a mixed bag - a typical catch that would show the type of fishing an angler could expect towards the end of the year. We also wanted to display the river in its best autumn raiment: it wouldn't, for instance, look terribly seasonal if we fished along a broad, treeless stretch of water, however vast the shoals: we would, therefore, cast and explore until we found the perfect combination of golden boughs and eager fish. We spent a week fishing, but not filming, around Standlynch Mill and, with the nights wet and the days bright, no rod was straight for very long. We caught lots of chub to over 4lbs, several roach to $1\frac{3}{4}$lbs, a couple of pike, a bucketful of unwanted rainbow trout and a score of dace. Hugh was obviously enjoying himself immensely, but I must confess to a slight twinge of regret at having to spend all that time fiddling with ridiculously fine lines and tiny hooks when I should, especially then, have been wielding a more powerful rod and dropping a big bait into a favourite barbel swim. It seemed misguided to toy with the proletariat when I could have been courting the aristocracy. But, as Hugh said, there would be plenty of time for barbel later on.

Hugh discovered a beautiful little hatch pool overhung by a yellowing ash tree and having caught several different species

'Perch love deep, quiet places out of the way of the current, amongst old piles'

there, decided it was an ideal location. Having an affinity with hatch and weir pool since childhood, I obviously agreed. There is always something exciting and attractive about the way the water surges in from above and then smooths seductively towards the pool's tail. Even the dullest, most fishless day on a quieter stretch of river can be enlivened by a cast into a hatch pool, where there is always something happening.

Above the hatches was a deep willow-bordered carrier that not only looked extremely picturesque but, as Bob soon discovered, also contained some very nice roach. Though completely different in character, our two swims were almost within casting distance from each other, making it possible for Hugh to keep a cameraman's eye on both floats at the same time. Bob's was the first to go under, yet while he'd found no difficulty in catching roach sans camera, now the focus was upon him he had to go and catch an out-of-season trout. I did even better. In the shaded depths beneath the ash tree I could see several chub, roach and perch all grouped enticingly together. As my float drifted over them I expected - and got - an immediate response. My rod curved over and, after a tussle, up came a great writhing eel. However, I fished on and eventually caught a handsome perch. It wasn't exactly a monster, being only just over a pound, but it had a sudden and completely unexpected effect on the proceedings.

As we looked down on the lovely fish, bristling among the fallen leaves, we all agreed that it was an archetypal sight, though we didn't actually use that word. 'Crabtree-esque,' we said, meaning that we associated it directly with the traditional angling scenes in our childhood bible, *Mr Crabtree Goes Fishing.* I quoted from memory: 'Now here's a typical perch hole. They love deep, quiet places out of the way of the current and against camp sheathing or amongst old piles. Perch fishing is stirring sport. It is a joy for the boy beginning to fish and equally so for the old veteran...'

As I slipped the perch back into his home we suddenly had the idea to make the scene not just redolent of Mr Crabtree , but alive with the real Mr Crabtree.

Though now in his mid-eighties, Mr Crabtree's creator, Bernard Venables, is still a tremendously enthusiastic angler. I have been out on the river with him a number of times and am always impressed by his endurance and his powers of concentration - the

intense, quiet concentration of an old heron. I knew he was still especially keen on perch and when we asked him if he'd join us in our autumn episode he said he'd be delighted.

We all met one morning, above the mill, where the river reflected an avenue of golden beeches and where Bob was sitting on a bench, waiting with a flask of his excellent tea. And, to complete the scene, he was also reading an original 1950s copy of *Mr Crabtree Goes Fishing*. Bernard enthused about the river, Bob

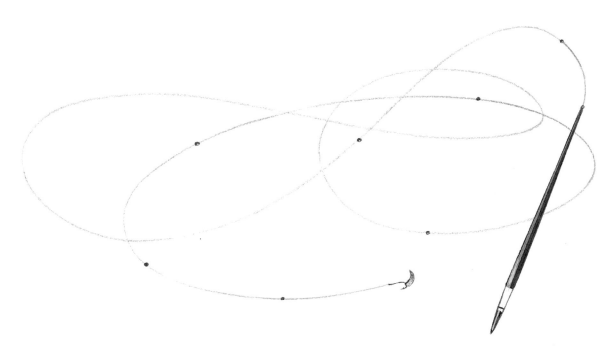

THE DELICATE ART OF TROTTING FOR ROACH

Float fishing skills are nowhere better demonstrated than by the roach angler 'trotting' the stream. After carefully considering the speed of current and depth of water, he will choose a float to match the conditions. Then he will precisely arrange the shot on the line so that the bait maintains the correct depth while also behaving naturally in the flow.

After casting, the float is delicately controlled by light finger pressure on the rim of the reel (a centrepin is the ideal winch for this game), allowing the bait to ride slightly ahead of the float and ensuring more natural presentation of the bait. This subtle technique can fool an entire shoal of roach into capture before the last - and often the largest - specimen wises up to the situation.

My own standard shotting pattern is illustrated. It always causes great hilarity with Hugh and Bob.

enthused about the book, I enthused about the tea and we all enthused about perch. There was a little dead-end carrier off the main river, a quiet backwater, neglected, overgrown with sedge, just the sort of place where Mr Crabtree would have expected perch. In fact Bernard's eyes lit up brightly as we led him there. He flicked out a worm on a size 8, using a lovely orange-coloured perch float and before he'd had time to settle properly on his stool the float bobbed and slid slowly away. Something was hooked and brought splashingly to the surface - a sparkling perch, about six inches long, the sort of prize that lit up our boyhood adventures.

The fish were in a frisky mood that morning for in seven casts Bernard caught seven perch, the last one putting a severe bend in his vintage rod (a 40-year-old Milwards Craftversa). After a dash into a clump of withered sedge and a dive to the far bank, Bernard brought a specimen over the net whose markings and colouration were almost dazzling. However, it was only a few ounces over a pound and, though Bernard was having a wonderful time, he agreed that, in the extraordinary world of Mr Crabtree, a perch angler would be expecting more extraordinarily-sized fish. Hugh had captured the right spirit, but now he suggested an abrupt change of scene, to a water containing perch that would astound everyone - even Mr Crabtree.

After the intimate atmosphere of an Avon backwater, the several hundred acres of Chew Valley Lake seemed like the Pacific Ocean. It was, of course, a famous trout water, but the previous year, on a quest for outsize fish, Hugh and Bob got permission for a day's coarse angling after hearing that the water also contained some monster perch. They caught a dozen between 2 and $3\frac{1}{4}$lbs which was probably the best perch bag of the season. So, as long as we could locate the shoal again, Bernard was sure to come up with another suitably extravagant specimen.

Hugh and Bob were obviously fairly confident of discovering the fish in the same area as before. They had made their catch by a wooden pontoon, used for mooring the trout anglers' boats, and as Bernard now cast again from that spot, they seemed to hold their breath. The orange-topped float bobbed in the ripples, but the minutes ticked past and nothing came to pull it under.

Bernard, knowing the way of big fish, was quite content to sit it out all day, but Hugh and Bob, who had caught all their perch

OVERLEAF: *Long trotting for roach along an avenue of willows*

109

within an hour, began to get restive. They suggested another casting place, but Bernard was only rewarded by a 3lb rainbow trout - unsurprising in the circumstances, but still disappointing.

'Gather ye rods together', said Hugh. 'If we all start fishing we're bound to find the perch somewhere.'

There was lots of action, plenty of bent cane and carbon, much screeching of reels, but only one perch. We lost count of the trout - brownies as well as rainbows - but only the cameraman, reliable as ever, hooked the required specimen. It was a two-pounder and as soon as it was landed we got Bernard to cast into the 'hot spot', while Hugh put aside his rod and hurried off to fetch the camera. The shoal, we thought, had been found at last.

Bernard's float soon sailed away, but when he struck another rainbow curved through the air. And so it continued, with enough trout to block the channel tunnel, until dusk.

It had been a long and active day and it says a lot for Bernard's energy and enthusiasm that he was all set next morning for another attempt. We fished a less exposed, more attractive stretch of bank, where willows and alders leaned into the margins and gave us some protection from the suddenly cool breeze. The place had a more 'perchy' air about it and we were pleased that the trout seemed to agree with us. We didn't see one all day. However, the first fish Bernard hooked was a 4lb pike. Then Bob, fishing right next to him, had a brace of pound-plus perch and I, fishing in the next gap in the trees, had a glorious specimen that must have been at least four inches long. At around noon there was general lamentation as Bernard hooked and lost a fish that we clearly saw and which was obviously over 2lbs. And then everything went very quiet and still and everyone stopped getting bites. Bernard fished on, his optimism undiminished, but I felt there would be no more chances.

The sun went down and a big yellow moon appeared in the eastern sky. There were only a few minutes of filmable light left but, when it was not quite too late, Bernard's float dipped and slid away and he hooked another good perch. It put up a dogged, deep-boring resistance, but Bernard, taking extra care this time, gradually brought it up through the depths and then a big, spiked dorsal broke surface. Bob reached out with the net and we all cheered as a handsome, hump-backed two-pounder was swung onto the bank.

Certainly a good perch, definitely a satisfactory end to the day's fishing - but again, not exactly the monster that Mr Crabtree might have expected. 'I know somewhere', said Bob, 'where the perch are even bigger than here.' Bernard just chuckled, thinking it best to humour the boy. But Bob wasn't entirely joking, and on the journey home we detoured to view a perch that would have made Mr Crabtree's famous pipe spout molten lava. It was 4lbs 10oz, a magnificent creature, gleamingly glass-cased on the mantelpiece of an old pub.

We raised our glasses to the fish, and then Bob, Hugh and I made a toast to Bernard, thanking him for imbuing our film with a bit of much-needed civility and authentic angling history.

On our next outing Hugh said we should, ideally, follow a 2lb perch with a 2lb roach and as we hadn't caught anything quite that size around Standlynch Mill, we'd venture upstream to the

It took us a week to locate the big roach, but they were well worth seeking out

RIGHT: *Harvest festival:*
Bob with his historic
catch of Avon roach, ten
of which weighed over the
magic 2lb mark

renowned big roach stretch near Longford Castle. However, as it was nearly thirty years since I'd fished for really large roach, I felt a bit out of my depth. This was definitely Bob's department, and though I spent a few days vainly searching up and down the river for the legendary shoals, I soon got waylaid by the sidestreams, weirs and carriers, where there were lots of fat chub eager for my baits. Bob and Hugh continued to search for the red-fins, but over a week passed before they located them. The water level had been falling considerably after another long, dry period and, as they eventually discovered, the fish had moved out of their traditional deep autumn haunts and up to a shallower section of river where it was joined by a swift-flowing sidestream.

One evening, Bob set himself up on the opposite bank from the sidestream and, using flake, took a big bag of roach, including one well over the magic 2lb mark. Early next morning, Hugh fished from the actual confluence, trotting a float so that it curved out and down into the main river. In the space of an hour he took the best catch of roach he'd ever had at a single sitting: four two-pounders with the best 2lbs 10oz. That confirmed it: the main roach shoal had definitely been discovered and, though it must have been painful to do, Hugh tore himself away and hurried off to find Bob.

Bob and I were half a mile downstream, having a break from fishing and trying to take each other's hats off with a frisbee. Hugh came chuffing suddenly onto the scene, caught the frisbee in mid-flight, did two somersaults, leapt into the air and said, quietly, 'I've just caught some roach.' He proceeded to explain what had happened and within a few minutes both roach-heads were hurrying back upstream with rods and cameras, leaving me with the frisbee.

Hugh had fished immediately downstream of the confluence but Bob chose to cast from just above, so that his legered bait, a large pinch of flake, could be better held in position. There was a definite crease in the surface where the two differently-paced currents converged and Bob wanted his bait to settle on the outside of this watery seam towards mid-river. He used a feeder loaded with soaked crumb and ground grilled hemp and, waiting until Hugh was ready to roll, dropped the tackle in the required spot.

Hardly had he put the rod in the rest than the whisker-thin

tip quivered and pulled suddenly round, signalling a bite. He struck and as the whole rod curved beautifully over, he knew it was going to be something special. And it was: 2lbs 6oz. On the first cast! He ignored a couple of tentative pulls, preferring always to wait for a decisive bite rather than risk nicking a fish and spooking the entire shoal, then he caught another two-pounder. Then one of about a pound, then another two-pounder. Then another! He began increasing the groundbait from ping-pong-sized to coconut-sized and he kept casting to the upstream limit of the baited area so that a hooked fish would not be drawn through the rest of the shoal.

Hugh was loading fresh spools as fast as a mechanic fits wheels on a racing car. He became blasé, wading out into the river to get some alternative low angles. Still the roach continued to feed, even though he must have been standing right amongst them. They were, admittedly, perfect conditions for fishing - still, overcast, misty and very mild - but neither Bob or Hugh had imagined anything quite as sensational as this. It was a roach extravaganza - a riot of roach. By tea-time Bob was bringing the fish over his net with an almost casual nonchalance, and by the time I strolled up to see what had been happening he'd landed ten two-pounders with the best one only a fraction below 3lbs.

Even though I'm no great roach enthusiast, I was, naturally, flabbergasted. It was certainly the best catch of big roach in recent years and one of the best ever on the Avon. Moreover, Hugh had filmed it all wonderfully, despite the rather dull, flat light. Bob looked like he'd just drunk a whole bottle of extremely good port, but of course that wasn't going to prevent us from visiting the local pub for a proper celebration. As he and Hugh packed up, just as the light was fading, I was allowed a cast into that miraculous piece of water and caught, at $2\frac{1}{4}$lbs, my biggest roach in 25 years.

After the historic roach catch, plus a short film sequence in another pretty hatch pool - a sequence enlivened more by me falling off a collapsing stool than by the actual fishing - we could, at last, go questing for a big barbel.

Though I can be unforgivably rude about bream, salmon, rainbow trout, pike and even roach (I don't even have to mention zander or catfish as most sensible people are already rude about them), I honestly appreciate all forms of angling and all species of fish. I like to think of myself as a complete angler, though the label adheres more readily to Bob than me. Yet there are only two species that truly obsess me: the carp and the barbel, like a double sun round which I constantly orbit. As we set off in search of gold I was like an undisciplined deerhound let off the leash in Richmond Park.

We knew the whereabouts of the barbel shoal that young Peter and I had pursued back in the summer but, though it contained a couple of fairly large fish, they were not much above 10lbs. With the emphasis on autumn monsters and with Isaak obviously smiling on us again we wanted more than just a moderately huge specimen. As Hugh said, 'What we really need in this final sequence is a record fish'. The Longford Estate water had long held a reputation for harbouring one or two immense but solitary barbel and Bob and I were obviously determined to find them. But there was a lot of river to search, much of it wide and deep, and with numerous overgrown sidestreams and carriers. We could fish where we expected to find big barbel but this was not as good as seeing the monster first. However, we needn't have worried. Not only had Isaak given us his seal of approval, but we also had, in Mike Trowbridge, the best riverkeeper on the Avon. One day Mike spotted a barbel that he estimated might weigh over 14lbs. It was accompanied by another that looked only a pound or two smaller. They were lying in a clear, fairly shallow pool next to a big weedbed, directly overhung by an old oak tree. The place was on the edge of a large marshy island and though you could reach it on foot via a plank bridge, it was much more appropriate to 'do a Swallows and Amazons' and go by boat.

The river flows by the end of Mike's garden where he always has his boat moored. Very kindly, he agreed to row us to the island, with the boat laden with rods and tackle (mostly Bob's), buckets of bait and all the camera gear.

It was a beautiful late October day as we drifted slowly along the tree-lined banks. The sky was cloudless and the sun bright on the amber-tinted foliage - perfect conditions for a voyage to the monster's lair. As Mike quietly rowed, Bob and I leaned over the side, looking down through the reflected leaves, hoping to see dark, barbelish shadows, but all we glimpsed were a few pike and

'Wading further out into the river, Bob tried to steer the fish towards him.' This was the pool pointed out to us by the riverkeeper, Mike Trowbridge, that held monster barbel

shoals of fleeting dace. The boat glided gently to rest under a massive chestnut and after we'd unloaded, Mike drifted off downstream, promising to meet us in the pub next day for his well-earned reward. He'd pointed out the oak under which the barbel lay and now Bob and I carefully scrambled up that tree until we were hanging right over the water.

There was a little depression in the river bed, no more than four feet deep, where the current just perceptibly slowed before picking up speed again over a stretch of weedy, gravelly shallows downstream. As our eyes grew accustomed to the shaded water we gradually discerned the vague outline of a fish, lying motionless on the bottom. I could just make out a wedge-shaped nose and an enormously long, thick back, greenish, with an up-peaked

We prepared for the first game of conkers we had played in - well - almost a year

dorsal and pectorals like elephants ears. Truly, the mother of all barbel. There were also at least three others. They were not as large as the matriarch, but they still looked well over 10lbs.

In his unseemly eagerness to be up the tree first, Bob had overlooked the obvious fact that, once we had spotted the fish, he would be the last one down - giving me just enough time to make the first cast. But before I could pick up my rod the scoundrel unpocketed his baiting catapult and, from halfway down the oak trunk, got me in the ear with an acorn. Naturally I couldn't let that pass without a suitable response and so I scythed the back of his head with a frisbee.

Another viciously accurate acorn was just about to be exchanged with a whip-handed conker when Hugh arrived on the scene to restore order. He'd been filming the boat from along the bank and thought it curious that we should be behaving thus in the presence of a river god. However, seeing the bank strewn with conkers, and knowing I still had one palmed, he suggested we settle the question of first cast with a traditional contest.

So we rummaged in our bags for string and a sharp, pointed spike and prepared for the first game of conkers we had played in, well, almost a year. And Hugh felt it might reveal something of the mind of the big fish angler if he filmed the event. I scored the first chip, making a nasty crack in Bob's chestnut and when he failed to make any impression with his next swipe it seemed he was surely doomed. Yet he survived my following thwack and came back with a surprisingly solid 'Stuka' (as we used to call this high and mildly unsporting hammer blow), which completely de-stringed me.

Naturally I complained to the referee, but my appeal was rejected and Bob strutted off down to the hotspot with me limping behind (I still haven't repaid him for that second acorn). I climbed the oak again as Bob chucked in a whole bucket of hemp, corn and chopped meat, and I saw the great fish stir in her furrow in the river bed, and watched her escorts begin to move this way and that as the groundbait came wafting down in the current. As they were possibly conscious of my presence I thought, after a moment, that it might be best if I was to slip off downstream and go in search of another group of fish. But apart from a few small chub and a grayling, there was nothing to cast at. In any case, I couldn't really concentrate as I expected to hear Bob's reel at any moment...

RIGHT: *Balancing act:
Chris teases a chub into
the net from a precarious
position overhanging a
little Avon hatch pool*

Meanwhile, Bob had baited up two rods, one with corn, one with luncheon meat, and cast out from upstream of the tree so that his legered baits swung round and settled in the required spot. Both rods were carefully placed in rod-rests. There must have been a highly charged atmosphere, knowing the barbel were moving around at the end of the lines, but the first thing to pull a rod tip round was a raft of floating leaves. Because of the nature of the current, a constant procession of fallen leaves and bits of old weed-stem was filing past in precisely the wrong place, continually catching the lines. This is always a bit of a hazard in autumn, making it sometimes very difficult to fish a static leger and Bob eventually retrieved one of the rods and kept the line from the other much lower in the water. After an hour there was a sharp rap of a bite which he struck at and missed, but he recast and almost as soon as the bait had settled the fish grabbed it more boldly and Bob hooked it. He realised instantly it was no barbel. There is an almost lifeless solidity when you first strike a barbel, but this fish swept quickly and erratically away in the manner of a chub. It was, in fact, quite a big chub, over 4lbs, but naturally Bob just scolded it for disturbing the pool.

The sun went down across the river, making all the leaves smoulder like hot coals. As it sank behind the valley's edge Bob guessed his best chance had arrived. Dusk and barbel so often go together. But apart from a lovely little wriggling eel nothing came to his bait and as the light went altogether, Hugh packed up his gear.

I came back upstream to see Hugh on his way (his car was parked across the fields), but neither Bob nor I wanted to stop fishing. Also Bob now allowed me to cast from just upstream of him, in range of both the hot spot and his flask of tea. So we fished on into the night, discussing the characteristics and mysterious habits of large barbel and expecting a lunging take at any moment. It must have been about 10 o'clock when Bob's rod curved suddenly over and he struck.

'What is it?' I hissed, thinking he must have hooked the giantess.

'I don't know,' said Bob, 'Here it comes. Drat! It's another eel!'

He reeled the eel in under the bank where it suddenly splashed quite violently and when we peered down into the dark water we saw that it had turned into a barbel. Not a small barbel

either. I got it in the net without any fuss and we laid it on the bank in a pool of torchlight.

It was a very ancient and rather crooked-backed fish that, in its prime, would have been a much more impressive specimen. But, though slightly disappointed by its performance and the fact that it wasn't the monster, Bob was still quite jolly about it. It weighed 10lbs 5oz and, at the time, was his first double-figure barbel.

We walked back to his house along a muddy, starlit riverside lane, and celebrated his catch with a glass of port.

The barbel were still there when we climbed the oak tree again next morning. But Bob failed to impress them with his baits, and fishing from downstream and casting up into the tail of the pool, all I caught was a dace. Again we fished into the night, but this time nothing happened. On the next day we decided to change tactics. We bought a gallon of maggots and fed them into the head of the pool. Then Bob waded out into the river and trotted maggot-baited float tackle down into the barbels' lair. I climbed the oak and watched the fish turning quite enthusiastically for the free grubs. Bob's float drifted into view and I shouted that two big barbel were directly in its line. But though they must have seen the bait, they didn't move for it.

After an hour or two of this, with no results, Hugh said he had to go off and do some float fishing of his own. It was so frustrating to watch and now all he wanted to do was fish for dace so that he could at least ensure that the float would regularly disappear. (A man of constant action is Hugh). While he was gone I sneaked downstream of the oak and, using a big bunch of maggots on a size 8 and just a single shot on the line, cast into the pool's tail and let the bait drift naturally in the current. Of course I had to be careful that my upstream cast did not catch the downstream limit of Bob's float run, but there were only a couple of minor incidents and they did not lead to another catapult battle.

After perhaps fifty casts I had a slow dragging bite and struck sideways, keeping the rod point low. Something moved no more than a foot, then sulked immovably on the riverbed. I kept the pressure constant but not severe and eventually the thing began to come down towards me. Then it started going round in slow regular circles.

'I've got one!' I shouted. 'And it's a big one.'

'Then get it out of the swim!' yelled Bob.

I shall never quite forgive him this reply, for though it didn't seem unreasonable at the time, in retrospect I should have guessed what it might lead to. I'd been quite prepared to patiently tease that fish down into the net and, as long as I didn't hustle it, it would have slowly and undramatically succumbed. But of course as soon as I unthinkingly applied maximum pressure the fish objected and made a tremendous run upstream, going past Bob and almost torpedo-ing him out of the water.

Some barbel! I'd seen a long golden crescent as it curved away and had the teeth-crunching realisation that this was not only the biggest barbel I'd ever hooked, it might be the biggest barbel ever.

After the long upstream rush it went through a weedbed in mid-river and then came sweeping down under the far bank. With the cane completely hooped and the centrepin getting hot, I managed to slow it and then stop it. The fish turned and with a great splash, barged into the far side of a dense bed of streamer weed. For a second I saw its tail and a sail-like dorsal, then it was still and utterly stuck.

Bob came hurrying down with the net and while he was asking where the fish was I did another very foolish thing. Instead of wading along and getting well down below the fish I stupidly tried to heave it up over the edge of the weedbed. The inevitable happened. We glimpsed something long and gold wallowing in midstream, but it was too securely cocooned in weedstems and a sudden violent tail swipe jagged the hook free.

I gushed out a few unprintable words and went off to chew a mouthful of conkers. Bob said 'Never mind' and Hugh almost wept when we told him. The next night a terrific storm swept across the valley. Gale force winds and torrential rain continued for almost 24 hours and when, finally, we ventured back to the island all the leaves had gone and the river was raging down like the Colorado rapids. Suddenly it wasn't autumn any more and so there had to be an 11 month intermission between casts.

OVERLEAF: *'Autumn on the Avon is always a happy experience.' Sunrise through an October river mist*

Prior to our next attempt, Bob spent a week baiting up the oak tree pool and by the time we all returned - in mid-October the following year - the barbel were swimming nicely over a bed of

corn and hempseed. The colours and tones were exactly as before and it was as if we'd only been away for a day. The weather was ideal, mild and overcast after a night of rain and our hopes were high. Though I hadn't actually seen any barbel there, I quite fancied a deep scoop in the gravel at the island's tail and I left Bob with the hotspot to himself. First cast, before I'd even reached the end of the island, Bob had a strong, confident take and hooked a fish that hung low in the current and only very slowly came upstream, keeping to the edge of the weedbeds. It surfaced, showing itself to be, incredibly, just what we wanted: a big, glorious barbel.

Wading further out into the river, Bob tried to steer the fish towards him, but it responded by swinging round and making a surging return under the tree. I heard the screech of the reel from 200 yards away, dropped my gear, and ran back up the bank. After a few tense moments, Bob began to retrieve line again, raising the barbel gradually towards the surface and easing it steadily over his

The barbel were moving nicely over a bed of corn and hempseed

big-framed landing net. I arrived on the scene just as he was heaving the great parcel of fish onto the bank. We carefully unmeshed it, revealing to the camera a fabulous example of bar-bus maximus. It weighed 11lbs 13oz, which was not only extremely satisfactory but also strangely coincidental as it was exactly 11 months and 13 days since we'd last filmed there. Hugh, who'd been beginning to lose faith in us after the previous attempt, was not only delighted but also - as I was - slightly amazed at the suddenness of the catch. It brought our autumn episode to an abrupt but perfect conclusion.

But though the filming was now completed, leaving Hugh free to begin the equally time-consuming task of editing, we did in fact all go back to the autumnal river, taking an artist with us. The event is certainly worth a mention.

It was in October, by which time Hugh had completed editing and track-laying on three of the six films and virtually finished another two. We had also decided to publish this book and while I was still fiddling with Chapter One, Hugh had written the open-ing section and Bob had got a couple of hundred of his sparkling transparencies together and the brilliant sporting and wildlife artist Rodger McPhail had been commissioned as illustrator. Actually, 'commissioned' is really the wrong word. Rodger is in such demand that he had to be persuaded to work for us and, as a bribe, we offered him a day's fishing.

Bob prepared the ground well beforehand, slipping daily out of the back door and down to the river to bait up a couple of swims. And not only the river. Rodger is, poor lad, primarily a game angler and the delights of barbel and carp fishing were almost unknown to him. So as well as baiting a barbel swim, Bob also got the carp in his local pond salivating over dog biscuits.

Rodger had a long drive down from his Lancashire home and so arrived at Hugh's house on the evening prior to the filming. This gave us all a chance to meet and chat and eat and drink and throw frisbees, putting Rodger in the right frame of mind for his big day.

The next morning was perfect - overcast, still and very mild, with the river running strongly after recent rain. We all met up at Standlynch Mill and walked over to the carp pond. Bob had already tossed in a few sackfuls of free offerings and the fish were visibly slavering on the surface.

Because Rodger was not acquainted with the mysteries of carp fishing, we'd offered to supply the tackle for the day and show him the (8lb breaking strain) ropes. Bob now handed him a deadly-looking 12ft carbon rod, already tackled up and baited, and moved into position with him, telling him to keep low behind the reed beds and just flick the bait into the margins, where a carp was sniffling around under the surface.

First cast, the fish rose up, snaffled the double-dog-biscuit and sank into the depths. Rodger, suddenly looking much more excited than he had been about carp fishing, struck and the rod swept into a high tensile bend.

The fish dived into weed, but was brought, splashing and churning, back towards open water where it circled for a few minutes before being persuaded to dive into Bob's landing net. Not bad for a first carp: $12^{1}/_{2}$lbs.

Artist, Rodger McPhail, with his gillies, Bob and Hugh, and his first-ever carp

'Right,' I said. 'Now you've got to do it properly,' and handed him my 11-foot split-cane Bishop and vintage centrepin. Hugh and Bob went off, laughing, to make a pot of tea back at

*Early morning, with
Hugh fishing on the
Avon*

the mill, while Rodger and I crept round the pond looking for
another fish. There was one on the edge of a big weedbed, visible only as a pair of large lips sucking eagerly through the surface
film. Unfortunately, with just a light bait on the line and no
knowledge of the Wallis cast, Rodger couldn't quite reach it. For
once, I was being the attentive gillie. I quietly took the rod and
cast towards the desired spot. But while the bait was in mid-
flight, the carp suddenly turned towards us and I had only to
check the spin of the reel to drop it gently right in the fish's path.

It took the biscuit without hesitation but, as I didn't want to
risk its immediate rejection of the bait, I stood heron-still until it
had submerged properly. I had to strike before I could hand the
rod back to Rodger. He tried to raise the tip, but it was dragged
abruptly down and a large wave bulged away from us, dividing
the weedbed.

'Hey!' said Rodger. 'This is even bigger than the first one!'
But the carp kept going and Rodger said he didn't want to put too
much pressure on this nice cane rod.

'Don't be silly,' I said. 'You couldn't break it even if you wanted to. Just clamp down now, the carp's deep in the weed.'

He clamped down and the fish came to a boiling halt; but before he began recovering line, everything went horribly slack. The hook had slipped.

'Lunchtime!' called Bob from across the pond.

After we'd eaten and taken a few of the photographic mug shots which Rodger needed for some of his illustrations, we set off for the river. Hugh, as ever, shot off towards the nearest roach shoal but Rodger said he wanted to catch a barbel. Before Bob took him down to his pre-baited swim, we said he should get in some 'training' with the local chub. Rodger had, in fact, caught chub before, but it was still a good idea to work gradually up to a barbel rather than crash straight in and probably get smashed straight up. We went round to a nice steady glide below a weir-pool where we could usually guarantee a fish first cast. After careful instruction, Rodger dropped a bait nicely in the approved spot, under the far bank. But the response was slow to come and when it did it was just a feeble pull which Rodger missed on the strike. He missed the next bite as well.

'Let's see you try,' Rodger said and Bob and I, needing no second telling, cast across. Bob used legered flake while I tried rolling a piece of bacon grill. It was the flake that was taken and Bob played in a richly-coloured four-pounder. 'Easy!' he said, and handed his rod back to Rodger.

Suitably impressed, Rodger cast again; he eventually got a firm nab-nab sort of bite to which he responded perfectly and in a minute or so he was the proud captor of another stunning-looking fish - the biggest chub he'd ever caught.

Rodger may have been enthusiastic about the idea of fishing the Hampshire Avon but he had, before we set out, been a little diffident about the species of fish we were actually casting for. Though his artistic eyes could appreciate almost everything that swam, like many anglers and non-anglers alike he felt that silver tourists (salmon) and spotty Herberts (trout) were the only things worth catching.

But after the carp and now the chub, he was enjoying himself more than he'd expected and could understand better our own particular passions. Suddenly he was seeing 'coarse' fish in a different, more golden light.

Bob led him down to the barbel swim, a lovely pool where a

great willow almost spanned the width of the stream and where the current slowed to a gentle meander under the near bank. Producing a packet of pongy pea-sized particles that went under the name of 'Marine Mix', Bob baited a size 8 hook and then, using a half-ounce leger, cast out to the edge of the trailing branches. Rodger sat down in a comfortable fishing chair, with the rod in the rest in front of him.

A few minutes glided expectantly past and then the rod tip just wheeled over. Rodger grabbed the butt and didn't even need to strike. Was it what we sought? It stayed deep and low and didn't dart about like a chub. Yes! It was a barbel, which Rodger brought, tussling and plunging to the net. He laid it gently on the bank and gazed at it in admiration. A fine six-pounder, with bright gold flanks, an olive green back and coral pink fins. And, thanks to Bob, another great first for McPhail.

Thus was Rodger's Avon initiation completed.

Afterwards, we fished our separate ways and each had a bountiful catch of chub and roach though there were no more barbel. At sunset we all reeled in and met at the nearest pub. When we reeled out again, at closing time, Rodger said, 'This has been a tremendous day.'

6

—

Midwinter Madness

OPPOSITE: *A Kennet sunset: 'The river like molten ore and the mist spread in dense layers across the fields'*

A freezing haze hung over the distant river and the south-eastern sky began to flush with the pale tints of a mid-winter sunrise. Bob and I trudged along a rutted track, hearing a weir's whisper become more clearly audible above the crunch of boots in icy puddles. Then the whisper rose to a roar and we came upon a white torrent of water where the river dropped six feet from a smooth glide above to the turbulent pool below.

As we stood watching the weir, our breath rising like smoke in the icy air, we spotted a strange five-legged monster moving between the bankside trees. It approached through river mist and gradually resolved into a hairy cameraman carrying a great wooden tripod.

'Morning Hugh,' we said.

'A perfect dawn for filming,' he said. 'But not quite perfect for fishing,' said Bob.

'Oh, I don't know about that,' said Hugh, 'A real expert could probably catch a netful.'

'If there was an expert here he might prove you wrong,' said Bob.

'As it is,' I said, 'we'll have to rely on luck.'

'As usual,' added Hugh.

Thus began our winter episode.

We were on a stretch of the Kennet above Newbury, where the river flowed through an attractive, well-wooded estate and where only trout anglers were usually allowed. Rising from the Marlborough Downs, the Kennet is the classic flyfisher's chalk-stream. But as well as trout, the water holds a marvellous head of big chub, grayling, roach, dace and pike and (though a rare species in the upper reaches) there were even rumours of the odd big barbel. We were naturally grateful for the privilege of fishing there, but the reason we were not wildly optimistic about our chances that morning was because the cold clear weather had only just begun. It moved in, with sudden frosts and mists, the previous evening, when Bob and I were fishing the weirpool for

'It was easy to see the graceful forms of grayling lying motionless in the slow current'

the first time. Bob caught a tiny dace, a gudgeon and a bullhead, and I didn't even get a bite. Winter fishing can be glorious on mild, soft days, but when the temperature drops towards zero it is better to stay in bed.

However, with the world rich in all those Christmas card elements associated with the season - sparkling frost, smouldering sun, bare silhouetted trees, ice, red noses - the morning made a reasonable curtain raiser, fish or no fish.

Bob began float fishing on one side of the weirpool and I began legering on the other. Bob prefers things to unfold in an orderly fashion. He was obviously pleased by the way the previous episode had developed and, keen to follow a similar course, began this winter programme in exactly the same manner - with an out-of-season trout. Luckily the Kennet is not noted for eels and my first bite resulted, instead, in a very nice chub of exactly 4lbs. But, though I expected further piscean activity, there was no more response to my baits. Likewise, Bob soon decided the weir was not as good as we'd expected, and, despite the cold water, was sure he could find a more productive stretch elsewhere.

He shouldered his gear and headed up the north bank, walking slowly along the deep slow glide and coming eventually to a marvellous pool on the outside of a bend. Most of the flow drove against the outside of this bend and continued its regular course, but a significant body of water wheeled back on itself and swirled slowly round a wide bight. Bob waded across to mid-river and, with Hugh filming from the bank, he began trotting a float down the crease between the faster and slower currents.

It was a classic float fisher's swim and Bob didn't have long to wait before he'd caught his first proper fish - a pretty silvery dace. Then a small roach, then another improper trout. He felt certain there'd be a shoal of chub under the line of downstream alders and so it proved to be.

Half an hour after Bob's departure, I too abandoned the weir and came upstream along the south bank to see how he was doing. As I approached the glide under the alders, my throat went dry at the thought of what might be down there and, though it was extremely bad manners, I couldn't resist crawling into position and casting a hookful of sweetcorn directly in front of Bob's float. He was using maggots which the fish obviously liked less than corn for, while the float remained floating, my rod tip

OVERLEAF: *Midwinter magic: A biting hoar frost casts its spell along the riverbank*

thumped over almost as soon as my bait touched the bottom. Into the net came a frisky, brassy 2½lb chub and as I held it up for Bob's disapproval he let fly with the baiting catapult. I could hardly complain, even though it was loaded with maggots.

I slunk off downstream again, leaving Bob in peace, and of course he soon caught a chub of his own as well as a good roach of about a pound and several more dace: in fact, he ended up with quite a large bag of fish.

We had fished the main weirpool but there was another smaller weir at the same level, marking the head of a backwater that rejoined the river about 300 yards downstream. There's something about backwaters and sidestreams that I've always found exciting and intriguing as they are usually neglected and forgotten and you never know what you might find lurking in the depths.

I had a few half-hearted casts into the little weir, and then explored further down, coming after a time to a bend where the current had scooped a deep hole out of the stream bed. This hole was almost completely overhung with a great bristling hawthorn that leaned across from the far bank. Its branches reached into the water and formed a dense half-submerged thicket. A more perfect chub pool would be difficult to imagine; in fact when he later came down to find me, Bob described the place as 'probably designed by Mr Crabtree'.

I managed to restrain myself long enough for Hugh to get quietly into position on the far bank, concealing all but the camera on the downstream side of the hawthorn, and then I crept up to the water's edge. Amazingly my first cast didn't go into the brambles and, even more incredibly, I got another instant take. Something snaffled my sweetcorn as it drifted down under the tree and the strike put an impressive bend in my old cane rod. But before I could get the fish out from his sanctuary, the hook sprang free and the line flew back into the tree behind me.

Hugh glanced up from behind his tripod, his expression a mixture of amusement and dismay. I made a muttered apology, rebated and cast again. Once more the corn was taken after only a few moments and this time I gave it an extra second before striking. The cane went into its not-so-familiar bend and this time the fish stayed on. I steered it down and out, keeping the rod tip low, then it surfaced and slapped the water with its tail. Another handsome chub came over the net after a bit of a flurry. More silvery than the others, it weighed just over 3lbs.

Hugh gave me a cheerful thumbs-up and withdrew from the scene as quietly as he'd arrived. The sun climbed to its low winter zenith, becoming warm enough to melt the frost on the grass and dry reeds, though the ground remained iron hard. The air was completely still and it was quite pleasant to sit waiting for another bite, with a few birds twittering nearby - robins, siskins and tits - and the stream sliding gently past.

Though I am a confirmed carp and barbel addict, there is something very appealing about chub fishing and many of my happiest angling memories concern 'sweet chavender' (or 'old loggerhead', depending on your point of view). The German name for him is dipkopft - blockhead. Winter or summer he will be enthusiastic about almost anything you care to offer - from a prawn to a piece of plum cake. He will also take a fly, wet or dry. The 'fearfulest of fishes', said Walton, but as long as you approach with caution and fish with care, the chub will usually respond. The grandfathers, however, seem to behave differently to their

The ground remained iron-hard, the air completely still, and a robin watched our every move

RIGHT: *Not even ice will quell the enthusiasm of a passionate angler*

smaller relations and can present an extremely difficult challenge. Yet it is the relatively undemanding nature of the fishing that makes ordinary-sized chub so agreeable: there is time to sit back and enjoy the delights of the waterside, and if you hook and lose a fish it is not a disaster, you will soon have another chance. Moreover those ordinary-sized fish are still a satisfyingly weighty quarry, averaging over 3lbs on a good river like the Kennet or the Avon. They are often beautifully coloured, have a strong, bold outline and a powerful build. The fact that they prefer closed-in, snaggy, overgrown retreats, like the one under the hawthorn, makes them not only easy to find but also provides an easy escape from the more conventional crowd, who only like fishing in open, uncluttered, unexciting places.

The rod tip jagged once and quivered. I struck, but missed. Rebaiting with three grains of corn (on a size 8) I recast, let the bait settle under the tree, then rested the rod carefully on the dead reeds.

It was an almost perfect morning, but the one element it seriously lacked was a cup of tea. Luckily my brewing-up gear was near at hand, and it wasn't long before I'd collected a few twigs and got the Kelly Kettle smoking like a train. Bob smelt the woodsmoke even before he'd spotted the familiar plume drifting over the trees; he reeled in, waded ashore and came striding down the bank to join me. But just as I was pouring the water into the teapot, a chub grabbed my bait. We heard the reel click and saw the rod twitching in the reeds.

I could have reached the rod, if I'd dived, but Bob was nearest and his conditioned reflex ensured that the cane was bending in his hand even before I dropped the kettle. I complained that it was my fish, but Bob reminded me of that other chub which should have been his. He brought it expertly over the net and I lifted it out. Another fine silvery specimen, and Bob deserved an extra biscuit with his tea. Had he not reacted so quickly then my beloved Lucky Strike might have been snatched into the river. But he was still guilty of poaching and as he slipped the fish back, I told him he didn't deserve any biscuits at all.

Hugh decided, after our tea, that it was time he did some fishing of his own. He was pleased with the introductory sequences but felt he might lose focus if he didn't soon cast a line himself. Bob also felt the urge to explore pastures new and the

two of them went upstream, where the river was deeper and slower, to search for monster roach.

I remained by the hawthorn and didn't meet up with them again until dark, by which time they'd had several glorious redfins to almost 2lbs and Bob had lost a lunker at the net. As usual, they had fished their favourite methods, Hugh using a float and Bob using the feeder. I, too, had caught a few roach, but only up to a pound. And I'd also landed five more splendid chub.

As it was over 50 miles to home and we'd got at least a fortnight's filming ahead of us, we had arranged to stay at a little riverside fishing hut on the Wilderness water upstream towards Kintbury. This had only been possible because Bob had a personal friend in the riverkeeper, Eddie Starr. Actually, Eddy is a good friend to us all, but it was Bob who first introduced him to us. When we got back to the hut he was waiting for us as he wanted to hear how we'd got on. So we invited him in for supper.

Eddie is a great character, with a wide knowledge of the river and a wealth of original ideas, not only about the keepering of trout - which is what the Wilderness is famous for - but also about the habits of fish generally. He harbours an understandable distrust of pike but has an encouragingly enlightened attitude towards the other natives of the river, species - like grayling, chub, roach and dace - that narrow-minded game anglers are traditionally hostile towards.

We had enjoyed some wonderful fishing on the Wilderness in the past and Bob had caught dozens of big roach and grayling. It was really because of the attractiveness of the weir that we'd begun our winter film down towards Newbury, but we certainly intended spending most of our time on Eddy's stretch, at least for the roach and pike.

However, though Eddy's grayling were very fine, they were even finer upstream at Hungerford. Grayling are in peak condition in winter, and they were an obvious choice for this episode. Therefore it was rather convenient that the riverkeeper at Hungerford was not only Eddy's younger brother, Rob, but that Rob was also Bob's son-in-law! (If you want good fishing, you need good contacts).

The frost was even thicker next morning, and not only were the grass and reeds white but even the trees, right up to their topmost branches. Ice fringed the river, and the only idiots up before sunrise had a similar fringe forming round their beards.

'A classic day for grayling,' said Hugh, as we looked at the water from a frost-covered wooden bridge. 'But an even better day for hibernation,' I said, and my words turned into a long trail of steam.

Bob and Hugh went up to explore the Hungerford water and I said I'd join them later on and hopefully take a few photographs of any specimens they'd caught. For the time being, though, I'd fish the deep glide above the bridge. Eddy had not only seen grayling there, but also a small shoal of dace that must have averaged a pound apiece. More importantly (though I didn't say this at the time), I'd be able to slip back to the nearby hut for tea and toast whenever my blood began to freeze (and I

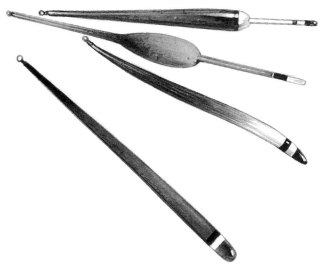

In the Company of Loafers, Bungs and Sliders

There are almost as many types of float as there are patterns of trout and salmon fly. They are the ultimate collectable for the coarse angler. Yet, I feel a float has only to perform two simple functions: it must allow the bait to be delicately presented and it must clearly signal a bite to the angler.

There are now so many variations of design - each one for a specific purpose - that I find it difficult keeping track of new developments. Although the angler really needs only half a dozen different types of float, he will find himself compellingly drawn to a tackle shop's display, so appealing are the colours and shapes. Soon he will fill his creel with those wonderful painted crow-quills, avons, antennas, wagglers, loafers, bungs, sticks and sliders. Here are a few of my floats. Bob and Hugh wouldn't be seen dead with any of them and tell me I'm out of touch.

guessed that would happen with monotonous regularity throughout the morning).

Rob Starr led Hugh and Bob down to a lovely-looking pool
called the Wine Cellar. It was situated on a gentle bend and was
over-shadowed by a huge and ancient willow. The water was low
and clear and they could easily see the graceful forms of a dozen
large grayling lying motionless in the slow current, fish which
weighed anything up to 3lbs and more. Bob decided to fish from
above the willow, allowing his light and delicate float tackle to
drift down round the tree roots and towards the rickety landing
stage beyond.

He baited with two maggots and, first cast, the red-topped
float slipped beneath the surface and he hooked a fish. It went off
in typical grayling fashion, deep and determinedly, but just as
Bob got the whole of his 12-foot rod arching above it, the hook
slipped out. The next bite resulted in a fast-moving, river-cleav-
ing and extremely unwelcome rainbow trout of almost 4lbs. The
grayling were decidedly unsettled after that, but Bob remained
patient, kept casting and was finally rewarded with a beautiful
fish of around 2lbs.

Anglers may wax lyrical about the lovely appearance of their
favourite species, be they salmon, trout or carp, but the grayling -
'the lady of the stream' - is irrefutably the most beautiful and
elegant of them all. In shape it is like a more delicate version of a
barbel - streamlined and slender with a down-curved nose. The
silver, exquisitely-marked flank is tinged with a faint purple that
turns, in the males, to a deep mulberry in springtime. Its final
glory is in the great furling dorsal, like a rainbow-coloured sail.

The fishing only gradually improved but, with the unthawing
winter landscape, the filming was successful from the start. Even
at midday, when I came upriver for a progress report, the ice was
still thick under the banks and the trees were still white with hoar
frost. I would have found Hugh and Bob sooner, but I met
Robbie first and, excellent fellow that he is, he pointed out an
inviting underbank pool where we could see a shoal of grayling
drifting in the flow. Of course I had my rod with me and naturally
I had to have a few casts. They nearly cost me my lunch.

A handful of maggots got the fish suddenly moving to the
upper end of the pool, just as my float tackle went down to meet
them. Rob and I held our breath, but all the grayling ignored the

bait. Next cast, the float darted under and I hooked a fish of about a pound which immediately got off. Robbie groaned and left me to it and of course I had to get one after that. Eventually I caught a half-pounder and, predictably, that wasn't good enough. After another half hour I landed a lovely fish of 1½lbs.

Then, naturally, I had to have several last casts and by the time I'd hooked and landed a big bruiser of a trout and another smaller grayling, it was almost too late. We just made it to the Toad and Trout before last orders for lunch.

Hugh filmed a lively incident in the afternoon, with Bob hooking another biggish grayling and me trying desperately to take a photograph of the action. As the fish lunged downstream I hurried along the bank to the old landing stage and, lying flat, tried to get a duck's-eye view through the camera. It was the sort of angled shot that Hugh knocks off brilliantly every time, even though he's wrestling with half a ton of Arriflex. With nothing but a simple box Bronica, I nearly fell in.

There had been the occasional drip-drip of melting ice after lunch, but just before sunset the temperature began to fall again and a chill mist started to rise and thicken. I went back to the Wilderness for a few final casts by the old wooden bridge and Hugh and Bob came down soon after to say it was time for tea. But the sunset was magnificent, with the whole western sky glaring like a furnace, then smouldering into a lingering powdery red. The river ran like molten ore and the mist spread in low dense layers across the fields. It was just as well Hugh always carries a few spare cans of film...

The fishing hut, which was made available to us by the generosity of an angler who fished for the Wilderness trout, was a bit of luxury. Not only was it well-heated, it had a kitchen, hot and cold running water, a lawn which ran right down to the riverside and a lane which ran 300 yards from the gate to a pub. Word soon got out that we were holed up there and every other evening we played host to a motley collection of itinerant fisherman, poachers, rod-builders and other riff-raff. These visitors soon realised they would be more welcome if they arrived with a bottle of port, which ensured a higher standard of conversation and a better class of frisbee game in the garden afterwards - always in the dark.

Naturally we spent a good deal of the long winter evenings discussing the progress of the film and thinking up probable and improbable developments to the plot. Eddy would regularly sparkle our eyes with tales of the great fish he had seen over the seasons and, of course, all these monsters were instantly incorporated into our saga. There was, said Eddy, an enormous pike, over 30lbs, lurking under a downstream weed rack, also a colossal chub, well over record proportions, skulking in a nearby pool and several specimens to burst the heart of any roach or dace enthusiast.

So, inspired by Eddy, encouraged by whoever else was present and emboldened by the port, our dream scenario went something like this: while Bob attempted to break the 3lb roach barrier, I went in search of superchub. Having attracted a shoal of monster rutilus, Bob unwittingly invited the attention of the mythic pike. Neither he nor I were wild about pike so we called in Eddy to catch it for us. Then Bob returned to the roach and realised his dream. And just before the credits rolled, I finally landed a goliath chub. The end.

Somehow or other this grand strategy led to an argument between Bob and Hugh on the superiority of their respective roach techniques. Bob favoured the leger while Hugh, as ever, championed the float. Eventually they decided to settle the issue with a wager. 'I'll bet you a bottle of vintage port,' said Bob, 'that I can catch a 3lb roach on the leger before you can catch a two-pounder on the float.' 'You're on,' said Hugh. (I should add that neither angler had ever managed either of these feats before on the Kennet).

By the time this challenge was proposed we had been on the river several days and the weather had changed a good deal. The high pressure system, with its frosts, mists, clear skies and numb fingers, had been shouldered aside by a big Atlantic low, which meant mild westerly winds, overcast skies, rain and normal-coloured noses. It also meant hugely improved fishing. On the morning after Bob's boast, the clouds were breaking, the sun was shining at intervals and the wind had dropped to a soft downstream breeze. After the usual breakfast of porridge, tea and toast - but taken much quicker than usual - we gathered our rods which were all tackled up from the previous evening and strode off to the river.

Hugh chose to fish a straight even-flowing glide above a line of hawthorns while Bob pitched into a deeper, slower pool, just above the pike-haunted weed rack. Hugh presented his bait - single maggot - on a size 20 hook and a needle-thin float, Bob legered two grains of sweetcorn on a size 10. Almost immediately, Hugh began catching dace, then grayling, then roach. He landed a good one, over $1\frac{1}{2}$lbs, by mid-morning and before noon he and his float had won the bet, with a fish of $2\frac{1}{4}$lbs. However, though Bob accepted this as a 'technical defeat', he suggested they should extend the challenge to the end of the day and then compare results. Unwisely, Hugh agreed.

Just after lunch Bob also caught a 2lb roach. As it seemed certain that something else would follow, Hugh stopped fishing and set up his camera. By then Bob was casting his baits just inches in front of the old wooden weed rack, a place where, despite the proximity of pike, he had often caught roach before. He was feeding a little mashed bread and corn into the swim, but the hours passed, it began to grow darker and his rod tip remained unmoved.

Hugh had just loaded his camera with faster film stock, because of the lessening light, when Bob's rod tapped once and pulled steadily round. He hooked a fish that stayed deep and simply plodded round in circles on the riverbed. Holding it clear of the tackle-shredding rack, he successfully steered it up and across and it rolled on the surface, just beneath his rod top. In the half-light there was a dull flash of a great silver flank. The net was readied and the fish came safely into the mesh and was lifted out. Bob gasped and called me up from downstream. 'And bring the big torch!' he shouted.

I burst through the dead reeds behind him and shone a beam on one of the largest and certainly the most beautiful roach we had ever seen. It was deep-bodied, high-backed, small-headed, with crimson fins and tail. The large, flawless scales had a wonderfully rich lustre of blue and gold across them.

It seemed almost outrageous to have to offend such a dignified, aristocratic creature by putting it in a bag and weighing it - but a bet is a bet. We all thought it was easily going to pull the needle past the 3lb mark, but it failed by a fraction of an ounce. However, the fact that Bob got his best-ever roach on the day after wagering he could do it, surely deserved a bottle of port

152

even if it hadn't quite made the mark and even if Hugh had already won his half of the bet. And as I had refereed the roach fishing, it was only proper that I also refereed the port drinking.

'That'll do for the roach,' said Hugh. 'But now we need a giant chub and pike to round it all off.' The next day, however, the weather deteriorated badly. Another cold front came in and the light went colourless and bleak. Then the skies filled with cloud and a tremendous wind began to rise. We managed to get home to our loved ones just before England was struck by the second major hurricane in four years.

Several weeks later, when we went back to the Kennet, we were quite surprised to find the old fishing hut still there and still in one piece. In fact, apart from a few trees lying in the water, there were hardly any signs of storm damage at all. The river was up a bit, which was to our liking, and we began fishing down by the weed rack again. The deepening glide above and the even deeper eddy below made it an attractive place for a variety of fish.

Though the big pike had often been seen there, Bob had also caught many good roach, several large chub and a near-record-sized dace. He felt he was still destined to break the three pound roach barrier and began fishing on the downstream side of the rack, in the slow eddy. I fished from about 20 yards above,

The chub: to me he is 'sweet chavender', to others he is 'old logger-head'

cramming seven grains of corn onto a size 6 and hoping for the grandfather of all chub. Hugh had the camera prepared, but said he'd only roll if something really extraordinary happened. In the meantime, he went off to fish upstream, though within hailing distance.

I had a bite first cast and missed it. But I got a second chance and hooked a fish that screeched the reel and almost made it under the woodwork downstream. Kennet chub fight much harder than their Avon brothers and it was several minutes before I worked the fish over the net. I could tell it wasn't going to be a monster, though it did turn out to be a very fine-looking specimen - a perfect chub of 4lbs 7oz.

After three more of almost exactly the same size, I said that Hugh should get ready, as maybe something remarkable was going to happen. Then Bob got a fish, too, not a roach, but another 4lb chub. I hooked a fish which plunged downstream and refused to come back up until I had followed it some way and applied sidestrain. This time, I thought, but no, it was another four-pounder, 4lbs 15oz to be precise. I got one more, of $4\frac{1}{4}$lbs, and then hooked something that didn't do anything at all except sit on the bottom and radiate gigantism. Naturally, it was the only one I lost.

Apart from a nice grayling, Bob had nothing more and Hugh managed a few medium-sized roach and dace, but was plagued by pike attacks.

Next day the pike were again active and, while Bob fished once more below the weed rack, both Hugh and I spent the morning float fishing with sprats. It was something I hadn't done in years and I quite enjoyed myself, even though none of the pike we caught weighed more than 7lbs.

Then Bob had his swim-feeder pike-snatched as he reeled in and he called me down to remove the shark from his pool. And as this was the monster's lair, Hugh set up the Arriflex, just in case. I was using a lovely big orange float that Bob had given me; just like a traditional Fishing Gazette pike bung. What with this and my old Hardy salmon rod and 8lb line, I felt ready for anything.

Within minutes, the float bobbed and was drawn inexorably down; I struck and the ancient cane curved over. But it was no leviathan. I brought it straight in and was just reaching for the net when the fish seemed as if it had decided to be a leviathan after

all. It made an unstoppable rush for the wooden uprights of the weed rack and I expected to see them splintered to matchwood as the beast crashed through. But nothing broke, not even the line; everything came to a rather disappointing and abrupt stop, with the pike firmly snagged.

I reeled myself upstream and hopped onto the plank that runs right across the rack to the far bank. When I was over the fish I wound down and heaved, but nothing budged. Bob, who had begun to fish upstream, came laughing to my assistance, thinking I had merely made a mis-cast round the woodwork. I assured him it was a pike I'd got, and a big one, and when he began to prod about with the net handle we could see something stirring in the depths.

The orange bung showed above the surface, and was then dragged down again. I let the rod take the pressure, then heaved, and up once more came the float. It started to go downstream and I presumed it would tow us and the weedrack behind it, but then suddenly all pressure ceased and up into the air jumped a little 3lb pikeling.

Obviously old snaggletooth had, in his cannibalistic manner, grabbed the little mouthful just as I was bringing it to the surface. But then, when someone clonked it several times on the snout with a net handle, it decided to let go. Amazingly the little fish was hardly marked and certainly not scarred.

'Cast again!' urged Hugh. 'He might try a second time.'

I cast, but the float rode unmolested on the calm surface and the monster refused to move again.

Next morning, another mild almost spring-like morning, I woke to find the hut strangely silent. Normally Hugh was always up at some dark, unsavoury hour, deliberately clanking an empty kettle around, trying to wake us up before he kindly made us a cup of tea. But there were no sounds and I wondered if - for the first time in the history of film making - Hugh had overslept. But he was not in his bed. And neither, astonishingly, was Bob. This was suspicious. Something untoward was afoot.

I made a quick cup of tea and, foregoing porridge, grabbed my rods and net and hurried down to the river. As I approached the weed rack the nature of the deceit became clear to me. There was Bob, in the place where I'd hooked the monster, and for the first time that winter he had a pike rod in his hand. Not only that, but the rod was bending inexcusably and, what's more, Hugh, the fellow-conspirator, was filming the action.

I arrived on the scene just in time to net a very hapless specimen of a pike. True, it was brilliantly marked, as if freshly-painted with gold and silver splashes over metallic green: true, it was 21lbs, twice as big as the biggest pike I've ever caught: true, I would never have landed it on my line. 'But you were poaching my swim!' I said. 'If you remember,' said Bob, 'I was fishing here first. And anyway I thought you didn't like pike.' 'Well,' I admitted, 'I would have quite liked that one. But I have to say, it wasn't the one I lost yesterday. It's not as big.'

Bob asked me to wait a moment while he went off to get something. I became suspicious again, but had to laugh in disbelief when he hauled in a big carp-sack containing another 20lb pike! He and Hugh had sneaked down at first light and done the deed even as I was still dreaming (about chub, of course, and definitely not pike. Well, only a little dream about pike, actually). This one was a 26-pounder and the brace made a tremendous sight, the sort of piscean pairing that makes even heretics gasp. They made a suitably triumphant end to our filming. And it was the end because, though I tried, I never did catch that record chub.

7

Monster Myths

LEFT: *'We believed the
legends but we wanted to
see some tangible evi-
dence'. Chris returning a
20lb leather carp to a
lost lake*

Stories of lost lakes never fail to stir my imagination and I am a sucker for even the most vague description of such places. By following the right set of clues I am always hoping to find my way to some half-remembered pool, where no-one has fished for ages and yet where there are rumours of monsters. In my mind this lake is always the same: deep, overgrown, mysterious, surrounded by tangled woods, a watery relic of some ancient estate whose only links with a more grandiose past are the ghosts - and the carp, who can live as long as elephants. My enthusiasm for this gothic fantasy will, if I'm spared, endure for the same amount of time. And though it is a fantasy it can, occasionally, become reality.

Of course, originally, it was just the carp alone that interested me; only later, when I began to discover more about them,

A special event in any carp angler's day: a hobby flashes low over the lake

did I learn about the lost lakes. As I read all the historic and contemporary carp literature, I kept coming back to the same kind of compelling descriptions of places where few were given leave to visit, let alone fish, where visions were reported of creatures as wonderful, terrible and mythical as anything in Loch Ness.

A lot of my time, probably far too much, has been spent on expeditions across some of the most beautiful parts of England in search of these lakes, and even today, when so much of the landscape is under threat by motorways and theme parks, the search continues. When I was a lad I thought I must have been slightly insane (my family thought I was completely insane). But no-one else I knew, not even the more enthusiastic fisherboys, were so bewitched by carp. Later on, however, my younger brother Nick joined me in my madness and now I realise there were, in fact, many others like us, who all dreamed the same dream and Bob was certainly one of them. Like me, Bob had a long list of lakes he'd visited or intended to visit and a shorter list of places that almost fulfilled his idea of perfection. Furthermore, he recently pointed out to me the location of a sublime lake I never knew existed (which became the subject of my book, *The Secret Carp*) and he also discovered the magical location for our last episode.

Originally, we thought it would be fun to complete the series across the channel and see if we could go out in a blaze of glory with a giant French carp and a case of champagne. It was true we had already filled an episode with carp, at Redmire, but though they were quite big fish, they were not exceptionally so. Hugh felt we should conclude with a real monster and, in France, there are lakes where 50-pounders are not remarkable. Of course we had talked many times before about the possibilities of discovering an unknown monster in this country.

Bob and I had described some of the lakes we'd explored in the past, but while several of them had been truly enchanted we felt the potential for a new carp colossus was unlikely. Bob even mentioned the Wessex pool that would, ultimately, become our location. As I said, he'd seen the water once before, but that was in winter, when the fish were lying low, and the carp were only local legends. But then, though we'd already written a brief outline of our French expedition, something remarkable happened, concerning the man responsible for the largest carp in Britain.

One day a visitor arrived at my cottage weighed down with a great armful of old, battered loose-leaf files. They contained the entire stocking records of the late Donald Leney, owner of the Haslemere Trout farm, going back 60 years to the time before monster carp were synonymous with his name.

When in 1980, I caught my 51-pounder from Redmire, Mr Leney, whom I'd not met before but knew by repute, sent me a jovial letter of congratulation and invited me over for tea. (Incidently, because it was his preference and not at all because he was formal in character, I still refer to him as 'mister' rather than Donald Leney). The breeding and stocking of trout were his main interest but, since boyhood, he'd always been especially fond of carp and he had a personal interest in the new record carp as it was he who had originally slipped it into Redmire as a fingerling, in 1934.

It was just one of an introduction of 50 little fish and they grew on to become the most famous carp colony in angling history.

RIGHT: *The exquisite lines of a classic common carp. How can any angler resist its enchantment?*

But there were other Leney-created colonies. Some I already knew of, many I learnt about during our numerous delightful conversations - he was wonderful company - and the rest I discovered two years after he died, at the age of 86, when his nephew delivered all his files. (In the few years that I knew him, Mr Leney had become a great friend and I shall always miss him. I once took Bob to meet him and Bob described the visit as his best-ever tea party).

It was a nice parting gift, a kind of potted history of one of the most knowledgable and certainly the most catholic-minded of aquarists. There were records of all his various watery activities, not just concerning the breeding and supply of trout and carp, but of every imaginable freshwater creature, from mayfly larva to golden orfe, watersnail to catfish. And there were the relevant places and dates, including that momentous day in 1934, when the carp went into Redmire, plus other equally fascinating snippets of carp history, for Leney introduced his fast-growing Galician carp to waters all over England. There was one lake in particular that intrigued me. Wasn't its name familiar? I showed it to Bob who confirmed my suspicion: it was indeed that Wessex lake he'd discovered a couple of winters ago. Leney had stocked it in 1935 with 250 carp of exactly the same strain as those in Redmire. Furthermore, said Bob, this lake was pure chalkstream-fed and rich in natural food. If Redmire could produce record carp from Leney's brew, then...

The result of all this was that in early June, Bob, through his old contacts on that particular estate, arranged for us to meet Harry, one of the keepers. Harry would tell us all we wanted to know about the lake and, if the potential was truly as great as we hoped, and if Hugh could gain the necessary permission to film and fish, then we would cancel the cross-Channel ferry. We met Harry in a local pub and the first thing we did, after shaking hands and buying him a drink, was to show him the Leney document. He was fascinated, but couldn't believe that any of that original stock was still alive. The progeny, yes, but not the ancestry. However, we said that if near-60-year-old carp were still swimming at Redmire, why should that not happen elsewhere?

But of course this was all academic. We needed to know from Harry the position now, regarding large and not necessarily ancient fish.

'Yes, there's a few big carp in the lake,' said Harry.

'How big?' we asked.

'Maybe as long as a 20lb salmon,' he replied, 'but I can't judge the weight of a really large carp as I've never seen one out of water. As far as I know, no-one has ever tried to catch one.' There was one fish in particular, he said, that he only occasionally saw and which looked very big.

'As big as this?' I said, showing him a photograph of my record fish.

He looked at the picture for a moment, made a mental comparison, and said his carp was bigger!

We quickly finished our drinks and Harry drove us in his landrover along a winding tree-lined lane, through an ivy-hung gateway and into an expansive and beautiful park. There were hay meadows full of wild flowers, great stands of beech and old yew, a stately but forsaken-looking house, and, behind the house, the lake - a long narrow lake avenued by huge majestic plane trees. It all matched the dream quite perfectly.

Harry stopped at the lake head, where the feeder stream entered. It was very shallow just there, crystal clear and dense with weed - starwort, mare's-tail, hornwort, but we still fully expected to see a giant carp straight away. Harry had rarely seen any fish in the shallows, however, and he took us along a track to about halfway down the lake, where there was an overgrown island off the far bank.

'This is usually where I see the big fellow,' he said. In fact he'd seen it there only about a fortnight ago. That was good enough for us.

It had become obvious from our conversations that Harry was not just a very observant man, but an honest one. And as it happened, almost everything he described concerning the lake and the carp turned out to be true. However, we still hadn't decided for certain whether to base our last film there, even though everything seemed to be leading that way, and even though we'd kindly been given permission for such a venture. We believed the legends but we needed to see for ourselves some tangible evidence. Harry left us on the lakeside and Hugh, Bob and I spent the whole of that summer afternoon looking for monsters.

The water was weed-choked everywhere, generally shallow,

but with the odd deep hole and, as these things are excellent for carp, they are also encouraging for carp anglers. We crept on down the lake, peering between openings in the trees, worming through willowherb and carefully wrestling across dense banks of bramble and hawthorn. We saw a trout in a clear space between weedbeds, then a shoal of small fish that we couldn't at first identify, but which turned out to be dace. We had never seen stillwater dace before. But then we realised that the lake was not,

Moorhens picked their way across the lilypads while the carp made their stems tremble

in fact, ever quite still. Such was the strength of the feeder stream that there was a constant, just discernable flow down towards the outfall. However, the dace - fish of quick streams - still seemed a mystery.

The carp were certainly a mystery. While Harry suspected there were only a small number of them, and though we had several acres of very weedy water to search, we were still puzzled by the lack of any visible signs. No sudden, slow ripples, no vague blueish shadows near the surface, no splashes or weed-suckings.

We approached the outfall, where the lake narrowed considerably and turned at right angles to itself, forming a deep, heavily-overgrown channel before cascading over a sill into a gushing, gravelly stream. The stream disappeared down a green tunnel of willows and creepers. Despite the rush of water, the atmosphere in the channel seemed more intense, what with the confined space, the great walls of foliage and the stillness of the air. It was a good place for our first sighting.

As we stood chest-deep in nettles and brambles, gazing into the water, we saw a vague movement to our left, coming round the curve in the bank. Something was approaching, deep down; but the light was perfect and suddenly a big purplish mirror carp materialised right under our noses. We each hissed some incomprehensible but appropriate utterance: Ahh! Gaah! Yiiy! And, just as we hoped, it had the Leney 'fingerprint', the distinctive line of large scales running the length of the flank, a sure sign of the Galician breed. It was not Harry's monster, though, and we put it at around the 25lb mark. An excellent first sighting, however, and we were even more impressed a few moments later when a glorious fully-scaled common hoved into view. He was much larger than the mirror, longer, deeper and wider across the shoulders - a magnificent golden beast who was quickly joined by an escort of half a dozen other big fish, though none was quite as imposing as he.

Bob and I stood, transfixed and hyperventilating, trying to ignore Hugh's whispered pleadings for us to get out of shot so that he could film the carp without us.

So we wouldn't be going to France and a few days later we loaded our gear - and our bicycles - into our vehicles and prepared to begin the new season, and the last episode, in a magical English landscape. We set up camp under the plane trees near the lake head. As Harry had said, there was an old punt moored there which would prove useful for fish spotting, freight carrying and, perhaps, even life saving.

We began baiting up as soon as possible, getting the carp accustomed to the pleasures of sweetcorn, boiled peanuts, maple peas, hempseed, dog-biscuits and various reeking paste balls that Bob had brought by the sackful.

Within a few days the fish were truffling terrifically. We climbed all the best vantage trees and saw the fish again, both

'In the evenings barn owls would waft through the trees close behind us'

RIGHT: *Ready for the off, the punt lay beneath the overhanging plane trees and by early evening we had prepared our rods and tackle for opening morning*

down at the outfall and up near Harry's island. We also spotted the great fully-scaled carp again, but though it would obviously make a wonderful catch, we knew it wasn't the holy grail we were looking for. Harry had even described this lesser monster and said that it must be the second largest - but not nearly as big as the real giant. In the lake's hierarchy, the fully-scaled fish was a bishop next to an archbishop, a general next to a field marshal, the Royal Yacht next to the Titanic. Also, the giant was solitary, while the others were more companionable. We scanned the surface with binoculars and powerful telephoto lenses, but we didn't spot anything truly lake-shattering. Not that we disbelieved the legend.

As well as an angler's paradise, the place was also a haven for bird watchers. Every day we saw kingfishers, herons, dabchicks, coots, moorhens and familiar and unfamiliar wild duck. We also had buzzards continually soaring overhead and three times we saw a hobby. In the evenings, barn owls would waft through the trees behind us and, once, we watched not a common but a much rarer honey buzzard flying up the length of the lake.

At midnight on 15 June, just as had happened at Redmire two years before, I launched a celebratory rocket and Bob popped open a bottle of champagne. But unlike that earlier time we didn't make our first casts in the dark. We had not cleared - nor were we going to clear - any conventional pitches along the bank. So that we wouldn't arouse the carps' suspicions, we wanted to keep everything as natural and undisturbed as possible (we hoped they'd presume the rocket was an ordinary meteorite). The fishing would consist mostly of stalking, creeping and crawling behind cover and only casting when a fish was absolutely ripe for the picking. Even in moonlight, that would present problems after dark, especially for Hugh. So when we'd finished the champagne we retired into the tent and filled our heads with dreams of monster carp.

In the half light of dawn, the first bird to announce itself was a wood pigeon, followed immediately by a liquid trill from a blackbird. Then silence again, but a precarious silence, soon to be broken by the massed voices of the full avian choir. In that quiet interim, however, and before I fell back to sleep, there came another less pleasant sound - the atrocious clanging of an alarm clock.

What a ghastly way to begin a day! I'd forgotten how awful that noise was, having given up such horrible devices when I left school 30 years ago. But early rising is one of Hugh's little indulgences and if we were actually going to be filmed blundering into the dawn then, he said, we needed an alarm clock. Bob and I thought a cup of tea might have been more appropriate.

Instead of toiling down the long track, carrying all our gear, we'd decided to load everything into the punt and drift gently towards our baited pitches. It was a more leisurely and interesting way of going fishing than walking and we could watch for suspicious stirrings in the weedbeds as we paddled slowly along. The rods and other equipment had been stowed the previous evening and all we had to do was drag ourselves out of the tent and board the punt without falling in.

There was just a thin mist coming off the surface, and as we rounded a reed-fringed island the sun appeared between distant trees. Halfway down the lake, we turned, stopped paddling and let the punt nose into the bank. Leaving our gear, we quietly stepped ashore and scouted along the margins, looking for fish.

After all the planning and imagining, all the discussions about the problems posed by the density of weed, the treacherousness of sunken trees and, not least, the camera angles, it was marvellous that, at last, we were actually going to cast. A first cast into a secret carp lake that had never been fished before! The idea was enough to make you froth at the gills. But when we peered into the first baited area - a natural clearing in the weedbeds - there were no carp to cast for; and yet on the previous evening half a dozen big fish had been nose down on hempseed and maple peas. We crept further along the bank to the next pitch, but again there was no-one at home. Eventually we arrived at the overspill channel and we presumed we would again suddenly come upon all the carp at once. However, apart from the flitting dace, the depths were deserted.

We sneaked quietly back to the punt for the bait buckets and, as we had done before, sprinkled the chosen areas with tasty offerings. Though we had spent days watching the fish in various different weather conditions, we weren't familiar with all their patterns of behaviour. Despite having favourite feeding and basking places, they tended to roam about unpredictably and a whole day could pass without even a glimpse of them.

It was like being Richard Walker and Peter Thomas on their first historic visit to Redmire in June 1952. Like them, we knew our water had tremendous potential. Like them, we had never fished the place before and could hardly wait to get a line in. Like them, we really had no clear idea what to expect.

After we had rebaited the various feeding areas we climbed to the top of one of the bankside trees and scanned the water for signs of interest. It was a long wait...

A breeze sprang up, sparkling the water and making the leaves quietly hiss. Perhaps that was all it needed, just a gentle stirring of the water, to wake the carp, for suddenly they appeared - or, at least, one did - a large dark shape cruising across a patch of

THE BOTTOMLESS BAIT BOX

There is almost nothing edible that a fish will not eat, as long as it is presented properly and the fish are hungry! But while some species can occasionally be a bit pernickety, others have a reliably catholic taste. Chub, for instance, have been taken on everything from cherries to cheese, and fried cod to fruitcake.

On the other hand, a truly wild barbel, whose natural diet has never been corrupted by the cunning angler, will sometimes disregard even the sweetest

earthworm if it is unused to it. Trout will often suicidally attack anything resembling food, which is why the trout angler, if he is to retain his sporting credentials, must fish for his quarry with a bait that is not edible.

Most of the fish in this book were taken on such simple baits as: bread, worms, sweetcorn, maggots, luncheon meat and - for carp - dog biscuits and sweet-smelling paste balls.

Cycling in the rain. Bob and Chris arrive in style at the giant catfish lake. Note the large umbrella, an indication of Bob's aversion to getting wet

clear water very close to the surface. We watched it gradually approaching from downwind until it came to the carpet of groundbait and scattered the dace that had gathered there. Then it sank down through the crystal depths and began to feed.

Within minutes several more fish began to appear and all converged on the free offerings. But who would cast first? We couldn't really share the privilege. Yet naturally we both felt we had a cast-iron claim for it and there was obviously not going to be any gracious deferment. It was too early in the season for conkers so, while we were still up the tree, we had to toss a coin. Sensing I'd called correctly, Bob, the tosser, feigned a drop. He said he could still see the coin in the margins and when he climbed down to get it he called 'Tails'! and expected me to believe him. Then he hurried off to fetch his rod and as I had nothing heavy to stun him with, I agreed to be the partial observer and perhaps even tell him when to strike.

With Hugh following every move in his viewfinder, Bob slipped through the willowherb and made a slow, easy cast to the edge of the weedbed. The freelined boilie sank to the bottom and within a minute a carp cruised into view and went straight down on it. There was no hesitation at all: the fish just scooped the bait up and carried on its way, making the line on the surface twitch and slide. No hesitation, yet there was a noticeable pause in the Earth's rotation. This was it. The first moment of contact was imminent. The carp wasn't a monster, but it was a good fish in the high twenties and, as Bob struck, there was a tremendous explosion of spray and it launched itself straight into the air. Substantial tackle had been employed: a beefy 12-foot carp rod and 15lb 'big game' line. The fish ploughed into dense weed and the line made sounds like a stuck door being forced open. The rod curved down almost to water level and the fixed spool reel gave out a series of sharp short squeals.

Then, after about 25 yards, the carp's progress was halted, though it was still pulling with astonishing power. Bob has landed scores of 20lb carp, many more than me, but he was rendered almost speechless by this one. Perhaps it was, in truth, much bigger than we thought. Maybe Bob guessed as much, which would explain his sudden nervous laugh and his plaintive question: 'Now what's going to happen?'

And suddenly, with no last desperate lunge or violent swirl, it was all over. There was just a gradual increase of pressure and then - with a faint 'Tsssh' - the line snapped.

Hugh kept rolling, I whispered something ungodly, Bob said, 'I think it's time for a cup of tea.'

Unsurprisingly, there was a very negative reaction to Bob's loss. In fact every carp in the lake went into a state of prolonged disappearance and the place took on a haunted, almost hostile air. We didn't think it would last, but it did and, despite our offerings, nothing returned to the clearings in the weedbeds or to the outfall channel. We set out in the punt and did, at least, see evidence of a fish, quivering the tops of the mare's-tails as it fled from our approach. Nothing else, though. And then, after several days, the weather closed in and turned wet, windy and quite cold. We went home and I'd never even had a cast.

During the stormy spell, Bob heard yet another improbable story about a centuries-old lake. This tale, though, didn't concern carp, but catfish - those rare, peculiar and, as Leney described them, 'bloody ugly' creatures. Catfish were only introduced into Britain in small numbers during the last 70 years or so and as far as I'm concerned, they are about as welcome here as black rats and Dutch elm disease. But Bob felt that the strange alien nature of the story, with a truly monstrous 'thing' lurking in a very elegant and stately English lake, would give a nicely surreal - not to say bizarre - twist to our film. And if we all agreed to it, we could have a few days' fishing there while the carp in Wessex hopefully forgot about us.

I was not enthusiastic, but Hugh thought the story, as long as it wasn't entirely fictitious, had great possibilities, even though none of us knew much about 'cats'. It's true, Bob had once caught a catfish in France and, ten years ago, I wrote an article for Angling Magazine entitled Big Cats, but that was about my experiences pursuing a giant tabby round the London docks (for an April edition). I certainly had no wish to wrestle with something that looked like a bewhiskered giant sea-slug, and certainly not one that was rumoured to be six feet long and which weighed about 100lbs. However, once Hugh had voiced approval, Bob was irrepressible. He found the whole abominable idea wondrously appealing. And unfortunately the legend was given credence after I'd phoned the man who'd seen and fished for the monster - Frank Gutfield.

Yes, said Frank, it was true. Furthermore, it was doubly true.

A classical temple and lawns: but we knew that gothic monsters lurked in the lake

And so twice as bad. For there were definitely two monsters. He'd even hooked one and lost it after an epic battle of several hours.

But Frank also told me there were plenty of carp in the lake, most of them long, lean wildies; therefore I could enjoy their company while Bob waited to be engulfed. Hugh managed to get permission for our venture (internationally famous film makers can prove useful) and we set forth for a week's fishing at the new location.

It was rather lovely and also rather odd, for the lake and the grounds were probably not unlike our carp lake must have appeared two centuries previously, before the trees had grown up and before the formal grandeur had become a wilderness. The catfish lake was smaller and more uniform in character - in fact, though the margins were reed-fringed and thick with weed and lilies, there were closely-cut lawns running down to the bank.

178

Bob set up with a great battery of powerful rods, using everything from squid to dead roach for bait. Frank had said we should be prepared for a long wait and so Bob had also brought a small library of angling books - not all of them, I'm pleased to say, containing references to catfish. I left him to it, sitting reading in his giant bivvy and, though it was pouring with rain, I fixed up my Barder carp rod and went stalking round the banks.

Immediately, I began to feel better about our expedition. A movement in the weed beds revealed the presence of a carp and a pinch of flake dropped near it produced a very welcome response. The line drew instantly taut and the strike connected me to a lightning-fast wildie that almost made my old Allcock Aeriel glow.

He was about 6lbs and was the first of several streamlined, darkly golden fish that we took on a variety of baits and methods. Hugh, in particular, had some great sport, fishing in the shallows with dangerously light float tackle. The largest carp was, however,

Window of opportunity: Bob waits for the carp to materialise from the weed

not a wildie, but an ancient-looking 16lb mirror. It had the
appearance of a waterlogged barge and took a double squid
intended for the big cat. Bob also caught numerous small pike,
but there was no sudden confrontation with something stupefy-
ing. There were several baits continually in the water, day and
night, but the monsters, if they were there, avoided them.

After a while, I think Bob began to suspect that the cats had
gone off to join a travelling circus. What had seemed like a good
idea gradually evaporated, but of course I was not exactly despon-
dent, even if it had been a bit of an anti-climax for Hugh. Even
after all this time, he still has a touching faith in our abilities to
bank monsters to order. Bob should have known better. And he
inevitably got the brunt of my 'serves you right' and 'call yourself
an angler' jokes as we rode home.

It was rather a blessed relief to get back to the Wessex lake a
few days later. Just as we hoped, the carp had decided to re-mate-
rialise and were actually drifting across the place in the weedbed
where Bob had come unstuck. For some mysterious reason I actually allowed him another cast without serious protest and, for the
life of me, I don't understand why. I could at least have brushed
his beard with a frisbee as he crept into position.

This time we were certain that the big fully-scaled fish was
there amongst the other 'lesser' mirrors and commons. But Bob's
first cast, perfectly positioned in a small hole in the weedbeds,
came to nothing, even though we could see several carp passing
close to the bait. He cast again, into a different spot, but again the
fish ignored him. It was tense - we fully expected sudden drama
at every next moment - but the morning became afternoon and
still Bob's line hadn't even been tweaked. The carp gradually
sank from our sight and disappeared again into their undiscovered
sanctuaries. But they didn't re-emerge the next day or the next.
Then the weather turned against us once more.

Summer became autumn and still, incredibly, the carp eluded
us. In fact I have still not had that first cast for them. They are
certainly a magical and unfathomable breed, especially when I
think how easily we were able to approach and feed them in the
close season. But our story is not yet finished, for it will continue
beyond this book's final page.

As I write it is winter and the lake is covered in thick ice.
Hugh is in Africa, filming eagles and leopards and Bob is probably

freezing on the banks of the Avon, fishing for grayling. But we are still holding on to the dream of that legendary fish, even if it is beginning to seem a little fragile now. We shall be back at the lake in June, however, when the season begins, by which time the carp will have forgotten us. And I shall have my first cast with a new cane rod that master craftsman Edward Barder has not even built yet.

But now, under the ice, probably in the deepest part of the lake, the colony of carp will be grouped together, semi-comatose yet not in a genuine state of hibernation. For if it becomes mild tomorrow and the ice thaws then the fish will almost certainly begin to stir and feed again.

Perhaps the wise old giant is down there with the others, perhaps it is lying elsewhere in the lake, maintaining the solitary existence that Harry described. Then again, perhaps it has died of old age.

Maybe it is Bob's destiny that he will break my carp record. Perhaps I'll break it myself, which would make me look rather selfish. But there is every likelihood that the entire carp coterie - right down to the smallest fish - will outwit us again.

One Last Cast

An Epilogue by Bob James

ABOVE: *'If we had fished at sea Chris would still have caught chub'*

We are four years older than when we started. At times I felt 20 years older, particularly on a frosty winter's day when Hugh woke us pre-dawn, post-claret, curry and port... I have seen more dawns in the last four seasons than in the 40 that preceded them.

Conversely, I have at times felt ten years younger: after breakfast, after some of those magic moments which we got on film, and after hearing those yearned-for words from the cameraman: 'it's a wrap'.

Did our childhood dreams change with the passing of years? No, I suspect the three of us never left childhood and, being anglers, we have certainly never stopped dreaming.

LEFT: *Bob seeking some bankside advice from his mentor Mr Crabtree*

Occasionally, I get an image fixed in my head: it can happen in my conscious hours or during a dream, sometimes both. If it is a nice image, I simply call it a premonition, then smile and wait. I am sure Hugh is also visited by these images. But for him they are not premonitions or a preview of experiences lying in store. For him, the image carries with it a sense of desire, of quest; not something to be left alone to unfold in the fullness of time, but a desire to be pursued.

This is when you see Hugh's talent for filming the unfilmable. His 'gift' is that he works twice as hard for three times as long as those who wish they had his 'gift'.

How near have we got to realising Hugh's original dream of conveying the essence of fishing? That is certainly not for Chris or me to decide, maybe not even for Hugh to judge. You must be our jury: if as an angler you have found our tale to be the next best thing to going fishing, or if as a non-angler you now understand or at least sympathise with our affliction, we'll be a happy crew. And if our efforts inspire just three youngsters to follow in our footsteps, to take our places and get as much from life through fishing as we three, then yes, the whole exercise was worthwhile, most definitely yes!

Regrets? Just one: we never got Hugh in front of the camera. The plan was there. Chris was to be trotting for roach but making a pig's ear of it (which I think within the profession is known as type casting!). Hugh would then be heard to offer advice or criticism, and at this point camera and rod were to swap operators... This would have been great fun and if you felt you knew what Hugh was best at, you would have been in for a surprise. Yes, he is pretty good with a movie camera, but he's an absolute master at trotting for roach.

The whole thing has been a marvellous experience, an enjoyable challenge and, to use the modern parlance, a good crack. Going to Redmire with Chris - the only thing he wasn't late for - was a wonderful privilege. Many famous fishermen and angling writers have been there, but Chris always seems to get closest to it and his gentle evocative words take his readers there with him. I am sure Redmire will always be thought of as Yates's.

Chris never seemed so comfortable at the rest of our venues as he had at 'the mire'. At some of the other locations, when Hugh pointed the camera at him, the words still flowed but not always the fish. The camera didn't exactly help Chris when it came to fishing, whereas I got an extra buzz from being put on the spot and *having* to catch. We even started calling Chris 'Chubby Yates' at one time, for no matter what species we were trying to film, he just caught chub! If we had filmed at sea he'd have caught chub! The number of times I heard Hugh's voice from across the water saying 'not another bloody chub, Yates.'

We all learned much from each other, although I wonder if Hugh and Chris's fishing has improved as much as my photography! And de-hatting a fellow without parting his hair - at 25 yards with a frisbee - now comes easy to us all. We've become unashamed experts.

A waterside companion who would always show us how to do it properly

185

Chris has that special gift of being able to explain to me why I enjoy something, he has that sort of mind! In the same way, his words can make an event more memorable in the recall than in the happening. Hugh has a similar ability with his camera. Not so long ago he made a film called *Tom's River*. As my wife Jan and I watched it on the television, Jan said 'I live there but I hadn't noticed that,' and 'does it really look that beautiful?' - such are his powers of composition. I have to admit that some of the images Hugh has captured in this series leave a lump in my throat. I was there when they were filmed and I know how he got them, but still I'm moved!

Perhaps the most surprising thing of all is that we are still fishing together, still drinking together, yes, still eating curries and passing the port between us. After all, four years is a long time to endure a moody, obstreperous prima donna, so thanks for putting up with me you guys! How did I feel about you two? Well, they say that a man with one foot in a bucket of fire and the other in a bucket of ice is 'statistically comfortable'. There were times during our term together when I was statistically comfortable. That said, it has certainly been the best 'job' I have ever had.

So much for the two characters I worked with. Now for some that I met during the filming. Torquil, the Speyside keeper, must be the most benevolent keeper I have ever met, his company is sheer joy. Tony, on the Kennet, was a man who can distinguish the trustworthy from the untrustworthy at 100 yards; thank goodness we passed that test. Harry, in Wessex, is a man who is considerate about everything and everybody that his life and work affect. When will these 'Johnny Come Lately' conservationists listen to men like him? Another great character we have all seen dozens of times on television, but whom I've now met in person, is Bernard Cribbins. His narration for our film is completely in tune with everything we have tried to achieve. Thanks Mate - I promise to take you fishing and put you in my best swim at least once a year for ever! Yes, that does include celestial carping!

In a recent interview Hugh said he harboured an ambition during the filming - in fact he still does - to actually get film footage of a record fish being caught by Chris or me. That could still happen! The fish is there, I have seen it, but I've chosen not to tell Chris. A breach of friendship? No, he wouldn't tell me...

*Sunset on the Kennet and
Bob prepares to
wind in*

Anyhow, Chris has caught monsters before, twice.

Just as Harry told us, this one is a loner, it's a mirror carp and it's absolutely huge. As I write, Hugh reckons we can have just two weeks - the last two in June - to fulfil this ambition. After that he must complete the editing of the film if he is to meet his delivery date to the BBC. Who knows? It may not even take two weeks! It may need just that 'one last cast.'

187

INDEX

swift 103
swim feeder 114

T

tackle, float 43, 124
   barbel 73, 74
tench 60, 62, 65, 66
   fishing 57
Thames 16, 17
Thomas, Peter 173
Thunder and Lightning 97
Toad and Trout, public house
   148

Tom's River 104, 186
Tony 186
Torquil 186
trotting (for roach) 108
trout 21, 137
   brown 79
   fishing 92
   rainbow 89, 104, 112, 146
Trowbridge, Mike 9, 117, 119
Tweed, river 81, 86

V

Venables, Bernard 15, 17, 21,
   106, 112

W

Walker, Richard 17, 21, 173
Wallis cast 73, 131
Walton, Isaak 28, 141
watersnail 162
water-soluble strings 37
whirlygig beetle 57
Wimbledon Park Lake 17
Wild, Graham 9
Willy Gunn 89, 97
worms 173